# All My Passions

## *A Comedy in Three Acts*

### By
### Vin Morreale, Jr.

*Cover Design by*
*Mandy Morreale*

ISBN 978-1-7347313-5-4

academyartspress.com

All Rights Reserved.
Copyright © 2020 by Vin Morreale, Jr.

## CAST

| | |
|---|---|
| **Everett Montague** | 67, a washed-up soap opera star |
| **Melissa Mulcahey** | 34, the show's hard-hitting producer |
| **Sebastian Evers** | 48, the show's frustrated director |
| **Hamilton R. Bennett** | 33, crusader for morality in media |
| **Eric Needleworth** | 18, the show's latest head writer |
| **Newman Forrester** | 58, the executive producer |
| **Wilkie** | 48, Mr. Forrester's assistant |
| **Brandy** | 23, A buxom nymphet |
| **Brick** | 29, The handsome stud |
| **Juanita** | 26, Everett's maid & love interest |
| **Juanita/Wanda** | 38, Juanita's replacement |
| **Juanita/Paulina** | 19, Juanita's next replacement |
| **Dallas Pittsburgh** | 40, A tabloid TV Host |
| **Pamela Kingsley** | 35. A mystery woman |
| **Eleanor Sweitzman** | 67, An old acquaintance |

## SETTING

The set and offices of *All My Passions*,
America's longest-running soap opera.

*FOR ROYALTY INFORMATION AND PERMISSION TO USE THIS PLAY IN A PERFORMANCE, PLEASE EMAIL VIN@ACADEMYARTS.COM*

# ACT ONE, Scene 1

*AT RISE. Lights come up on a living room in a well-appointed mansion. Tiffany lamps and a loveseat dominate Center Stage. An Upstage door leads off to the kitchen and bedrooms. A grand piano is placed Upper Right, on top of which rests two fluted glasses and a silver ice bucket holding a bottle of champagne. Upper Right hangs a portrait of a proud and handsome gentlemen and Upper Left is a curtained window looking out to the gardens. The Stage Right wall has French doors leading to off-stage rooms. EVERETT, a 67 year-old playboy trying desperately to look 25, stares dramatically out the window, Stage Left. He wears a smoking jacket and a terribly unconvincing toupee. He is the same man as in the portrait on the Stage Right wall, only a great deal older. Lost in thought, he does not see JUANITA tiptoe silently through the Stage Right door. Juanita is an attractive young woman in a revealing French maid's outfit.*

JUANITA.   Oh, Mr. Everett. I'm sorry. I... I did not know you were home.

EVERETT.   Actually, Juanita. I was waiting for you.

JUANITA.   For me, Mr. Everett?

EVERETT.   Yes, Juanita. Would you like some champagne?

JUANITA.   No, Mr. Everett, sir. If Mrs. Everett were to find out...

EVERETT.   Mrs. Everett will not find out. At this very moment, Mrs. Everett is visiting her nephew Alfie in Seduction City.

JUANITA.   She is visiting Mr. Alfie? But Mr. Everett, Mr. Alfie is...

EVERETT.   Dead? Yes, I know. Pruned to death by the Japanese groundskeeper after he was caught having an affair with the little man's wife amongst the rhododendrons. Amongst? Among? *(Shudders.)* Either way, a horrible business. Poor Alfie looked so much like a Bonsai tree, they had to close the casket at the funeral service.

JUANITA. *(Steps closer.)* Poor Mr. Alfie.

EVERETT. Yes. A ghastly business. But you see, Mrs. Everett didn't think I remembered Alfie was dead, because it happened while I had that nasty bout of amnesia after Meredith's ex-husband pushed me out the window in a failed attempt to take over Everett Industries.

JUANITA. Poor Mr. Everett.

EVERETT. Yes, Another ghastly business. But I did recover to see Meredith's ex-husband brought to justice, and Meredith marry my step-son, Luke.

JUANITA. Lucky, Mr. Luke.

EVERETT. Yes. A happy business.

JUANITA. But where then is Mrs. Everett?

EVERETT. My wife? At this very moment, she is in the arms of her lover… *(Points to someone in the audience.)* Ferdinand Alcoa!

JUANITA. *(Aghast.)* Her lover?

EVERETT. Yes, her lover. She believes I do not know, but I do, and it tears out my grievously wounded heart. My wife thinks me a fool. And that is why I stare sullenly out this window at the lush lawns and sculpted grounds of my palatial estate.

JUANITA. Poor Mr. Everett.

EVERETT. All I ever wanted out of life was several billion dollars and a woman I could love forever. *(Sighs.)* Is that so much to ask? Yet, none of my seven wives have remained faithful. Each of them used my many trysts and tawdry affairs as a pitiful excuse for their own infidelities.

JUANITA. Poor, poor Mr. Everett.

EVERETT. Yes, poor me. And that is why I turn to you now, Juanita…the only woman I completely trust *(Touches her arm. She shudders with excitement.)* How long have you worked in my house, dear child?

JUANITA. Seven years. Seven very happy years.

# ACT ONE, Scene 1

*AT RISE. Lights come up on a living room in a well-appointed mansion. Tiffany lamps and a loveseat dominate Center Stage. An Upstage door leads off to the kitchen and bedrooms. A grand piano is placed Upper Right, on top of which rests two fluted glasses and a silver ice bucket holding a bottle of champagne. Upper Right hangs a portrait of a proud and handsome gentlemen and Upper Left is a curtained window looking out to the gardens. The Stage Right wall has French doors leading to off-stage rooms. EVERETT, a 67 year-old playboy trying desperately to look 25, stares dramatically out the window, Stage Left. He wears a smoking jacket and a terribly unconvincing toupee. He is the same man as in the portrait on the Stage Right wall, only a great deal older. Lost in thought, he does not see JUANITA tiptoe silently through the Stage Right door. Juanita is an attractive young woman in a revealing French maid's outfit.*

JUANITA. Oh, Mr. Everett. I'm sorry. I... I did not know you were home.

EVERETT. Actually, Juanita. I was waiting for you.

JUANITA. For me, Mr. Everett?

EVERETT. Yes, Juanita. Would you like some champagne?

JUANITA. No, Mr. Everett, sir. If Mrs. Everett were to find out...

EVERETT. Mrs. Everett will not find out. At this very moment, Mrs. Everett is visiting her nephew Alfie in Seduction City.

JUANITA. She is visiting Mr. Alfie? But Mr. Everett, Mr. Alfie is...

EVERETT. Dead? Yes, I know. Pruned to death by the Japanese groundskeeper after he was caught having an affair with the little man's wife amongst the rhododendrons. Amongst? Among? *(Shudders.)* Either way, a horrible business. Poor Alfie looked so much like a Bonsai tree, they had to close the casket at the funeral service.

JUANITA. *(Steps closer.)* Poor Mr. Alfie.

EVERETT. Yes. A ghastly business. But you see, Mrs. Everett didn't think I remembered Alfie was dead, because it happened while I had that nasty bout of amnesia after Meredith's ex-husband pushed me out the window in a failed attempt to take over Everett Industries.

JUANITA. Poor Mr. Everett.

EVERETT. Yes, Another ghastly business. But I did recover to see Meredith's ex-husband brought to justice, and Meredith marry my step-son, Luke.

JUANITA. Lucky, Mr. Luke.

EVERETT. Yes. A happy business.

JUANITA. But where then is Mrs. Everett?

EVERETT. My wife? At this very moment, she is in the arms of her lover... *(Points to someone in the audience.)* Ferdinand Alcoa!

JUANITA. *(Aghast.)* Her lover?

EVERETT. Yes, her lover. She believes I do not know, but I do, and it tears out my grievously wounded heart. My wife thinks me a fool. And that is why I stare sullenly out this window at the lush lawns and sculpted grounds of my palatial estate.

JUANITA. Poor Mr. Everett.

EVERETT. All I ever wanted out of life was several billion dollars and a woman I could love forever. *(Sighs.)* Is that so much to ask? Yet, none of my seven wives have remained faithful. Each of them used my many trysts and tawdry affairs as a pitiful excuse for their own infidelities.

JUANITA. Poor, poor Mr. Everett.

EVERETT. Yes, poor me. And that is why I turn to you now, Juanita...the only woman I completely trust. *(Touches her arm. She shudders with excitement.)* How long have you worked in my house, dear child?

JUANITA. Seven years. Seven very happy years.

EVERETT.  And during all that time, have you ever seen such a broken man? Such a wounded heart? Such a passionate soul in torment?

JUANITA.  No, Mr. Everett. That is why…I have always loved you!

EVERETT.  I suspected as much, Juanita. Now, won't you join me for a glass of champagne?

> *(He moves to the piano, Upper Right and pulls the bottle of champagne in an ice bucket. He opens the bottle and fills two fluted glasses.)*

JUANITA.  Yes, sir, Mr. Everett.

EVERETT.  No need to be so formal, Juanita. You may call me Everett now.

JUANITA.  *(Her inhibitions released.)* Oh, Everett, my darling. How I have longed for this moment! Finally able to reveal my true feelings! How my heart has burned for you these past seven years.

EVERETT.  *(Handing her the champagne.)* To us, my dear. And the wonderful future we shall share as husband and wife!

JUANITA.  To us!

> *(They toast, sip the champagne. Juanita grabs the glasses and places them on the piano.)*

JUANITA.  Now then…you and I have seven long years to make up for! Come to me, you dear, kissable man.

> *(She backs Everett to the loveseat. Everett gulps, then succumbs to her passionate embrace.)*

EVERETT.  My love! My darling! My... wooooooaaaaahhh!

> *(As Everett attempts to dip her with a passionate kiss, his aging back gives out. The two tumble behind the loveseat in a tangle of awkward limbs and screams.)*

JUANITA.  Aaaaaaaaaaaaarrrrrrrrggghh!!

> *(As she falls, Juanita grabs his toupee and it comes off in her hand. Her flailing arm the only thing visible above the loveseat.)*

EVERETT.  Yeeeeoooww!

SEBASTIAN. (OFFSTAGE) Cut! CUT!!

> *(SEBASTIAN enters through the audience and leaps onstage. Sebastian is a handsome, middle-aged African-American with gray streaks in his ponytail. The frustrated director runs to the loveseat and tries to help the dazed Everett to his feet, ignoring Juanita completely.)*

SEBASTIAN. Everett! Everett, are you all right?!!

> *(Everett's head pokes up from behind the loveseat. Half-dazed and missing his toupee.)*

EVERETT. I'm not...thure...

JUANITA. *(Jumping up.)* He bit me!!

SEBASTIAN. What?

JUANITA. That creaky old dinosaur bit me!!

SEBASTIAN. Where?

> *(She points to a set of false teeth attached to her bottom.)*

JUANITA. On my butt!! His teeth fell out and I sat on them!!

EVERETT. *(Toothless.)* I theem to have mithplathed my dentureeth.

JUANITA. Dentures, my butt!

EVERETT. Tho it theemth.

> *(Sebastian helps Everett to his feet. Then yanks the dentures off Juanita's butt. She yelps.)*

SEBASTIAN. Are you okay, Everett?

> *(Sebastian hands Everett his dentures. Grimaces as he reinserts them.)*

EVERETT. Not entirely. I may have soiled myself in the fall.

SEBASTIAN. Not a problem. We'll have costuming get right on it.

EVERETT. Apparently, actresses aren't as light as they used to be.

JUANITA. Say what?!

SEBASTIAN. Juanita will try to be more careful, Everett.

JUANITA.  *I'll* be more careful?!

> *(Sebastian tries to discretely wave Juanita to silence, in order to placate the aging star.)*

SEBASTIAN.  Thanks, Marie. That's all we ask. *(To Everett.)* Don't worry, Everett. It could happen to anyone. But no harm done. *(Straightens Everett's clothes.)* Are you up for doing the scene one more time?

JUANITA.  Not with me, you won't!

SEBASTIAN.  Now, Marie... Why don't you just calm down and we can...

JUANITA.  I'm through, Sebastian! You can find yourself another Juanita Modesty! My agent says he can have me playing a brain surgeon on General Brothel next week. No stupid accent. No skimpy French maid outfit. And I wouldn't have to kiss any washed-up old fossil!

EVERETT.  Washed-up old fossil? Whomever is she referring to?

SEBASTIAN.  *(Innocently.)* I have no idea, Everett.

JUANITA.  You need combat pay to do a love scene with this guy! Whose brainstorm was it to have my character fall in love with Mr. Viagra here anyway?!

> *(ERIC scampers on, Stage Left. The eager young scriptwriter is 18, sporting horn-rimmed glasses, and bursting with nerdy ambition.)*

ERIC.  That would be me. And um...my brainstorm.

JUANITA.  Who's this guy?

ERIC.  Eric Needleworth. New Head Writer for *All My Passions*.

EVERETT.  When did we get a new head writer?

ERIC.  Last week. After I graduated from high school.

EVERETT.  High school? Precisely what qualifications do you have to write for my show?

ERIC.  My Uncle Newman is Executive Producer.

EVERETT.  Newman Forrester? How many relatives can that man possibly have?

JUANITA.  If he's as horny an old goat as you...

SEBASTIAN.  Now, Marie...

JUANITA.  ...it could number in the trillions!

EVERETT.  I choose to take that as a compliment.

JUANITA.  Bite me.

EVERETT.  Apparently, I already have. And your expansive derriere seems to have misaligned my dentures.

*(She takes off her high heels to throw it at him, but Sebastian catches her in mid-throw.)*

SEBASTIAN.  Easy, Marie.

ERIC.  As I see it... Everett Montague has been the star of *All My Passions* for more than forty years.

EVERETT.  Forty-nine, to be precise.

ERIC.  Forty-nine years. I felt it was time to shake things up. Give him a new love interest. So naturally, Juanita would...

JUANITA.  No. Naturally Juanita, will not! I'm outta here!

SEBASTIAN.  Marie, please...?

JUANITA.  Dose up on reality, Sebastian. You're a great director, and I love working with you. But that clogged artery is the reason this show is now the lowest-rated soap opera on daytime television!

SEBASTIAN.  C'mon, Marie. Everett is more than a star. He's been with *All My Passion* since the beginning. He's an icon.

JUANITA.  Well, take it from your thirteenth different Juanita Modesty... That icon...and your show...are both on their last legs.

EVERETT.  Last legs?! I'll have you know I have slept with more women than I can remember!

JUANITA.  Big deal. That could be one.

SEBASTIAN.  Look, Marie. How about if we take your character in a whole new direction? We could have Juanita win the lottery. Then make a play for Everett Industries herself.

ERIC.  Or maybe she can have an affair with the Boston Red Sox? A different player every episode!

SEBASTIAN.  Not helping, Eric...

JUANITA.  I'm sorry, Sebastian. *All My Passions* is going down the drain. And I, for one, have no intention of going down with it! Oh, and here's your icon... *(Tosses the rumpled toupee at Everett.)* Looks like he's good for another four seasons.

*(She storms off, Stage Left. Eric follows her offstage.)*

SEBASTIAN.  Marie?!

EVERETT.  *(Adjusting his toupee.)* She seems upset?

SEBASTIAN.  *(Sighs.)* I guess that's a wrap, folks.

LIGHTS DIM

*(Begin cheesy THEME MUSIC. A single spotlight picks up a news desk rolled on, Stage Right. Entertainment reporter, DALLAS PITTSBURGH, 40 and plastic, sits behind the desk, with flawless hair, slick delivery and a too-perfect smile.)*

DALLAS.  Good evening, America! Welcome to another edition of *SOAP OPERA INSIDER*. I'm your host, Dallas Pittsburgh. *(Smiles too broadly.)* Well, it looks like another big slide for *All My Passions*. Just released network ratings show the geriatric soap stumbling along on increasingly wobbly legs. The writers finding it hard to breathe new life into Everett Montague and the gang at Seduction City. To make matters worse, the daytime icon has recently become the target of a national consumer boycott by an organization calling itself Americans For A Rebirth Of Values...

*(MUSIC FADES and lights dim, as the news desk is rolled offstage.)*

*(A single spot illuminates a man, Downstage Left. He yawns at his laptop computer propped up on a cheap TV tray. HAMILTON BENNETT, 33, has the rumpled innocence of a grown-up choir boy. He sits in his bathrobe, reading the letter he has just composed.)*

HAMILTON.  Okay, two-fifteen in the morning. Let's see what we've got... *(Reading off the computer screen.)* To Newman Forrester, Executive Producer. Studio City, California... Dear Mr. Forrester, this is my seventh letter in as many weeks, which should be proof that my commitment to this cause is as firm as ever. *All My Passions* remains a swamp of perversity in an industry seldom known for its high moral landscape.

*(He stands and recites from memory.)*

HAMILTON.  Our organization, Americans For A Rebirth Of Values, will continue boycotting *All My Passions* until your show either improves its moral content, or is dropped from the network schedule. We have already succeeded in convincing three of your sponsors...

*(A second spot illuminates a desk, Downstage Right. Corporate dynamo NEWMAN FORRESTER, 58, paces a narrow circle, as he reads the same letter aloud to a very nervous WILKIE, 49, his perpetual yes-man.)*

FORRESTER.  *(Reading.)* ...Finger-friendly Dishwashing Liquid, Pre-drool Toys and the Geriatric Security Underwear Company...to dump *All My Passions* in favor of more family-oriented programming. *(Looking up at Wilkie.)* Can he do that?

WILKIE.  It... um, appears he already has, Mr. Forrester.

FORRESTER.  Chickenhearted corporate types! Only interested in pushing their products! They have no appreciation of bigger issues. Like ratings, dammit!

WILKIE.  Yes, Mr. Forrester.

FORRESTER.  Shut up, Wilkie.

WILKIE.  Shutting up, sir.

FORRESTER.  *(Reading.)* ... Please understand that...

> *(A third spot shines, Upstage Left, illuminating MELISSA MULCAHEY, 34, vibrant producer of All My Passions. Melissa is an extremely attractive young woman, despite her cutthroat business demeanor. She continues reading her copy of Hamilton's letter.)*

MELISSA. *(Continuing to read.)* ... I am not disputing your right to air such morally bankrupt programming. I am simply asserting our right to object to this daily deluge of reprehensible filth. *(Fuming.)* Who does this guy think he is?!! Nobody messes with my filth!

HAMILTON. *(Continuing to recite.)* The Constitution gives us the right to curse our parents, define live sex acts as art, or broadcast grisly details of mass murders to young children. But just because we have the right to do these things doesn't mean we should succumb to such base exploitations...

FORRESTER. Who is he to say what I can and cannot exploit!?

WILKIE. Who indeed?

FORRESTER. Shut up, Wilkie.

WILKIE. Shutting up again, sir.

FORRESTER. *(Reading.)* It is not that *All My Passions* is the worst show on television...

> *(A fourth spotlight snaps on, Upstage Right. In its pool of illumination Sebastian, the director from the previous scene, sits on the piano bench and reads aloud the same letter to Eric, the eager young writer.)*

SEBASTIAN. *(Continuing to read.)* ...but it has been going through a terrible decline, ever since the episode where Everett Montague was sexually assaulted by a rabidly obsessed raccoon on a crowded Seduction City subway.

ERIC. That was one of my best scripts!

SEBASTIAN. Chill, Eric. Nobody else is claiming ownership of that one...

FORRESTER. *(Reading.)* Perhaps your show merely reflects the accelerating decline of modern culture...

HAMILTON. *(Continuing the sentence.)*... Yet, it must also recognize its contribution to that decline.

MELISSA. *(Continuing the sentence.)*... You have helped create a nation of drooling, lust-addicted voyeurs.

SEBASTIAN. You know, I kind of like the way this guy writes.

ERIC. *(Defensively.)* I can do better...

FORRESTER. *(Reading.)* We are all affected by what we see in that window. If we were not, than the billions of dollars companies spend on television advertising would be in vain.

WILKIE. He does have a point there.

FORRESTER. Zip it, Wilkie.

WILKIE. Already zipped, sir.

MELISSA. *(Reading.)* Philosophical arguments aside, Americans For A Rebirth of Values...

HAMILTON. ...plans to continue our boycott of *All My Passion*...

SEBASTIAN. *(Reading.)* ...until the show cleans up its act...

FORRESTER. *(Reading.)* ...or is ultimately forced off the air.

HAMILTON. Very truly yours, Hamilton R. Bennett...

FORRESTER. *(Reading.)* ... Americans For A Rebirth Of Values.

WILKIE. He's a nutcase.

FORRESTER. A whack job.

MELISSA. A fruitcake.

ERIC. A Fascist!

LIGHTS DIM on Hamilton

FORRESTER. So what do we know about this Hitler R. Bennett anyway? Any dirt I can use against him?

WILKIE.  Nothing I can find in the police records, FBI files, or sleazy Facebook links. He seems to be squeaky clean. Sells advertising for a small-town radio station. Doesn't drink. Doesn't smoke. Doesn't gamble. He even drives an electric car.

FORRESTER.  What about women?

WILKIE.  *(Refers to his notes.)* He was engaged to one…Joanna Jacobs. Engaged for three years, it seems.

FORRESTER.  And?

WILKIE.  Died eighteen months ago. Car accident. He hasn't dated since.

FORRESTER.  Let me guess. He started this Americans For A Rebirth Of Values after she kicked the bucket?

WILKIE.  Well, actually…

FORRESTER.  He's no longer getting his jollies, so he makes sure no one else will either!

WILKIE.  That seems rather harsh, Mr. Forrester. After all, his fiancée…

FORRESTER.  I like harsh. Harsh is good. Harsh is honest. Harsh is what made me what I am today! And you know what that is, Wilkie?

WILKIE.  Um…harsh?

FORRESTER.  Damn right, I'm harsh! Now go get Melissa Mulcahey on the phone!

*(Wilkie pulls a cell phone from his pocket, hits 'speed dial' and hands it to Forrester. Upstage, a PHONE RINGS, and Melissa pulls out her own cell phone.)*

MELISSA.  Yes, Mr. Forrester?

FORRESTER.  What are you gonna do about this Hamilton Bennett character?!

MELISSA.  Um…do, Mr. Forrester?

FORRESTER.  I've been on the phone with the network three times already!

MELISSA.  I imagine they're a little concerned.

FORRESTER. Concerned? They're two exits past concerned and halfway to Coronary! What with the declining ratings, and now this boycott, the big boys are running scared. They're talking about pulling the plug!

MELISSA. They can't do that! *All My Passions* is television's longest running soap opera.

FORRESTER. Yeah, and they say it's running out of steam. You're my producer. I want to know what you plan to do about it!

MELISSA. I'm not really sure what we can do. I mean it's not like we can have him killed. *(No reply.)* Uh…you do know that's still illegal, Mister Forrester?

FORRESTER. Your point being?

MELISSA. Illegal is bad. We need to come up with another option.

FORRESTER. No, you need to come up with another option. Call me back in an hour with a solution! Or it's back to game show hell for all of us.

*(Forrester throws the phone at Wilkie. Lights dim on Forrester and Wilkie.)*

MELISSA. Yes, Mr. Forrester, I... *(Looks at the disconnected phone.)* Great. One hour to save a show that's been dying for decades. Thanks a lot, Mr. Hamilton R. Buttinski!!

*(Melissa redials. Upstage, a PHONE RINGS. Sebastian picks up.)*

SEBASTIAN. Sebastian here.

MELISSA. Not for long. I just got off the phone with Forrester. You read the letter?

SEBASTIAN. I'm assuming he wasn't thrilled.

MELISSA. You guess correctly. For some reason, the expression 'swamp of perversity' didn't sit too well with him.

SEBASTIAN. Funny. It looks so impressive on my resume.

MELISSA. He gave me one hour to respond. No, not respond… one hour to solve this problem.

SEBASTIAN. Gee, that's a shame, Melissa. And here I am just heading out the door...

MELISSA. Oh no, you're not! I'm the producer. But you're the director. If *All My Passions* bites the big one, we're both out of a job.

SEBASTIAN. Maybe it's for the best, Melissa. I've been with this show so long, even I'm starting to believe that Everett really could be a babe magnet.

ERIC. Well, there is a certain…elusive mystique about the man.

MELISSA. Who the hell is that?

SEBASTIAN. Another one of Forrester's nephews.

ERIC. Are you talking about me?

MELISSA. Gopher?

SEBASTIAN. Head writer.

MELISSA. Just what I need.

ERIC. Is the show's producer really talking about me?!

SEBASTIAN. Ratchet down a game level, kid. This is big people talk.

MELISSA. I've spent too many years of my life and given up far too many relationships to make it in this industry. And I'm not about to let some megaprude from Dustmop, Indiana take it all away from me!

SEBASTIAN. Don't take it personally, Melissa. His kind pop up every now and then. He's probably just another Hollywood wannabee. For all his talk about values and morality, what he really wants is to be in television. Psychologists call it 'genius envy.'

MELISSA. You think that's all it is?

SEBASTIAN. I'd bet money on it. You give a guy like that a director's chair with his name on the back…let him watch a few days of shooting and make a few comments…and he goes back to Mayberry happy as a clam. Tells all the locals back home he was King of Hollywood for a day.

MELISSA. Sebastian, you're a genius!

SEBASTIAN. That's what I tell everybody. *(Suspiciously.)* Only you're the first one to ever swallow it.

ERIC. Swallow what? What did she swallow?

SEBASTIAN. Try not to speak, Eric.

MELISSA. You gave me the answer, Sebastian!

SEBASTIAN. Uh...I did?

MELISSA. Let me call you back!

*(Melissa runs out as LIGHTS DIM on her office.)*

SEBASTIAN. *(To Eric.)* Evidently, I'm a genius…

ERIC. Will it advance my career any if I agree?

SEBASTIAN. Promise me you'll never reproduce.

ERIC. Sure. No problem.

*(LIGHTS DIM on Sebastian and Eric. LIGHTS RISE on Newman Forrester and Wilkie, now with Melissa.)*

FORRESTER. You want to what?!

MELISSA. Don't you see? It's perfect!

FORRESTER. This seems to be a definition of 'perfect' I've never confronted before.

MELISSA. Trust me on this.

FORRESTER. Listen, lady. In Hollywood, we all know the phrase 'trust me' is Latin for "Castration with a smile."

MELISSA. Sorry, Newman. I don't buy the cynical routine. You're way too cuddly for that.

FORRESTER. Call me cuddly one more time, and I'll see you never work in this town again!

# ALL MY PASSIONS

*(She blows Forrester a kiss and exits. Forrester nods to Wilkie, who dials his phone. On the other side of the stage, the LIGHTS RISE again on Hamilton and his cat, Aquinas.)*

HAMILTON. *(Into phone.)* You want me to what?

WILKIE. *(Oozing sincerity.)* Think about it, Mr. Bennett. Instead of merely complaining, this is your chance to exert a real positive influence on the show.

HAMILTON. But I've never worked in television before. I wouldn't know what to do!

WILKIE. We have researched your background. You sell time for a local radio station in Indiana, don't you?

HAMILTON. Yes. But it's only a small...

WILKIE. Well, television is exactly the same as radio. Only with pictures.

HAMILTON. That's the only difference, huh?

WILKIE. Pretty much. Anyway, we know your time is valuable and we are more than happy to compensate you for your services.

HAMILTON. Compensate me?

WILKIE. Of course. We can pay you… *(Watches Forrester hold up ten fingers.)* Ten dollars…. *(Forrester shakes his head angrily. Draws three zeros in the air.)* I mean ten thousand dollars a week for your...um, valuable input.

HAMILTON. Ten thousand dollars a week?!

WILKIE. And we'll even throw in a credit on the show. Story editor... Script consultant...or something like that.

HAMILTON. A screen credit? For me?

WILKIE. You will work directly beside Melissa Mulcahey, our rather attractive, yet-to-be married producer. She's looking forward to meeting you. So what do you say, Mr. Bennett?

HAMILTON. I'm not sure. I'll have to think about it.

WILKIE. You do that. Mr. Bennett. You do that.

*(Hamilton and Wilkie hang up simultaneously. Hamilton looks a bit dazed.)*

FORRESTER. Well?

WILKIE. *(Smiling.)* Hook, line and sinker.

*LIGHTS DIM on Forrester and Wilke.*

HAMILTON. *(Picks up his cat.)* Well, Aquinas... Looks like I'm headed to Hollywood...

AQUINAS. Meow?

BLACKOUT

# ACT ONE, Scene 2

> *AT RISE: Lights come up on the same living room set as the opening scene, except that instead of an ice bucket on the piano, there is an elaborate candelabra. Melissa leads a wide-eyed Hamilton on a tour of the studio from Stage Right. Sebastian goes over script notes with Eric, Stage Left.)*

HAMILTON.   So this is where it all happens…

ERIC.   *(Whispers.)* Check out 'hick-boy.' He looks like he suddenly woke up and found himself in heaven.

SEBASTIAN.   This is better than heaven, Eric. This is Hollywood. It's heaven with residuals.

HAMILTON.   I still can't believe I'm really here.

MELISSA.   It is a bit imposing, isn't it, Mr. Bennett?

HAMILTON.   Like taking a bus tour of Sodom and Gomorrah.

ERIC.   Must be the local hot spots in Indiana.

> *(Hamilton looks at Melissa with undisguised wonder, as they cross to Center Stage. The others follow.)*

MELISSA.   As you can see, the show maintains four temporary sets and five permanent ones… Everett's office at Montague Industries, Vera's Brothel, the Critical Care Ward at Seduction City Hospital, and of course, Everett's bedroom. And here we are on the living room set at the Montague estates, where most of *All My Passions* is filmed.

HAMILTON.   But it's not technically filmed anymore, is it? You shoot on 4K digital video. Standard three camera set-up, from the looks of it.

ERIC.   *(Under his breath.)* Looks like hick-boy has done his homework.

HAMILTON.   Not only that, 'hick-boy' has excellent hearing.

MELISSA.   Uh… well, in Hollywood, 'hick-boy' is a term of respect.

HAMILTON.  Like 'trust me?'

*(Everett saunters in from Stage Left. Melissa grabs the aging actor, shoves him toward Hamilton.)*

MELISSA.  Everett! I would like you to meet Hamilton Bennett. Our new story consultant.

HAMILTON.  Story editor.

MELISSA.  Whatever.

EVERETT.  Pleased to meet you. I am Everett Montague.

HAMILTON.  I know. I've watched the show. And your real name is..?

EVERETT.  Excuse me?

HAMILTON.  Your real name?

EVERETT.  I don't follow..?

HAMILTON.  Not your character name.

EVERETT.  Whatever is this man babbling about?

*(Melissa pulls Hamilton out of earshot of Everett.)*

MELISSA.  Everett's real name is Everett Montague.

HAMILTON.  You named the character after him?

MELISSA.  No. Actually, his real name was Albert Mooney. But he had it legally changed about thirty years ago.

SEBASTIAN.  He's been doing the character so long he really believes he is Everett Montague.

HAMILTON.  Isn't that all a bit...scary?

SEBASTIAN.  It's a whole lot of scary. Sometimes, he'll sleep all night on the set, thinking it's really his mansion.

MELISSA.  Last month, he scared one night shift security guard so badly, she had to have emergency bladder surgery.

*(Everett, whose hearing is not the greatest, reacts to the hushed discussion around him.)*

# All My Passions

EVERETT.  Pardon me, but in my home it is not considered polite to whisper in front of the host.

HAMILTON.  I'm, uh, sorry, Mr. Montague. We were discussing your name.

EVERETT.  Yes, Montague. Did you know there is a character in one of Shakespeare's plays who also used my name?

HAMILTON.  Romeo.

EVERETT.  *(Frowns.)* You should know I do not respond to that kind of flattery, young man. No matter what the tabloids might say.

HAMILTON.  I only meant...

EVERETT.  I'm sure you did. And I am flattered. But I simply do not share your inclination.

HAMILTON.  No, sir. I meant the character's name was Romeo. From Romeo and Juliet. "What is a Montague, it is neither hand nor heart..."

EVERETT.  Huh?

MELISSA.  They have Shakespeare in Indiana? I'm impressed.

HAMILTON.  "A rose by any other name would smell as sweet."

EVERETT.  You can smell my feet? I was so sure I put on clean socks this morning...

MELISSA.  Everett also has a bit of a hearing problem.

EVERETT.  At least I assumed it was this morning...

HAMILTON.  A pleasure to meet you, sir.

EVERETT.  The pleasure was all mine, son. Although, I would rather you didn't call me Romeo again in front of the ladies. Bad form, you know.

HAMILTON.  Uh... yes, sir.

EVERETT.  Now then, Where is Marta? No wait... She was my fourth wife. Or was it my sixth? Juanita? Juanita? Where the devil are my clean socks?

*(Everett disappears through the Upstage Center door. Melissa moves closer to Hamilton. He is clearly entranced by the beautiful and intelligent producer, and she enjoys the effect she has on him.)*

MELISSA. Now you know the real secret of *All My Passions*.

HAMILTON. It looks like he lost *All His Marbles*.

SEBASTIAN. Why can't you write lines like that?

ERIC. I can. I'll have it in tomorrow's script!

*(They continue the tour as they all walk off, Stage Right. A moment later, BRANDY enters the set from Stage Left. Brandy is 24, blond, and stunningly attractive. A moment later, BRICK enters, Stage Right. Brick, 30, is a tall, dark, incredibly handsome man, with a chest as big as a Buick.)*

BRANDY. Oh, Brick!

BRICK. Oh, Brandy!

*(With every line, they take a step towards each other, though they remain a room apart.)*

BRANDY. Oh, Brick.

BRICK. Oh, Brandy.

BRANDY. Oh, Brick... I feel like I've known you forever... even though it has only been an hour since we first met at Little Bab's Bat Mitzvah.

BRICK. An hour can be an eternity to people in love.

*(They rush into each other's arms.)*

BRANDY. How can our passion be wrong, when it feels so right?

BRICK. Who cares what people think? What do they know of our love? Why should it matter if you are really the step-daughter of Everett Montague, and therefore my own half-sister by his first marriage to Chamberlain?

BRANDY. Or that you are undergoing treatment for sex-addiction and are wanted in seven states for both bigamy and philatelism.

*(He turns toward her, touches her shoulder.)*

BRICK.  Or that, only last year, you had a torrid affair with my uncle, my nephew, and virtually every other man in Seduction City.

BRANDY.  But I've changed now, Brick. I am no longer a mindless nymphomaniac...

*(She steps back, pulls off her blouse to reveal a sexy camisole bearing an American flag.)*

BRANDY.  *(Suddenly serious.)* I have my reputation as a US Senator to consider now. And you know that sex and politics don't mix.

BRICK.  *(Smiling.)* Tell that to the Democrats.

*(They kiss with passion.)*

BRANDY.  Oh, Brick!

BRICK.  Oh, Brandy!

*(They pull apart.)*

BRANDY.  Besides, the truth is...we have already slept together many times before.

BRICK.  *(Stunned.)* We have?

BRANDY.  Yes. Before you had that terrible bout of amnesia.

BRICK.  I had amnesia?

BRANDY.  Don't you remember?

BRICK.  Not really. Was I any good?

BRANDY.  You made my top twenty.

BRICK.  Well, let's see if I can move up a notch or two...

*(He moves towards her and they kiss passionately. She suddenly shoves him away.)*

BRANDY.  Wait, Brick. Before we make wild passionate love again... *(Turns her back to him.)* I have something important to tell you.

BRICK. Something important? That sounds serious.

BRANDY. It is. *(Turns to face him.)* It's...it's about... Dakota's baby!!

*(Brandy turns to face him with extreme melodrama. From offstage, an organ hits a DRAMATIC MUSICAL STING. Brick shrugs and sits down on the loveseat. As he does, Brandy's expression changes to one of confusion.)*

BRANDY. I said...It's...it's about...Dakota's baby!!

BRICK. Yeah. I heard you.

*(Brandy is confused by his lack of reaction. She screams.)*

BRANDY. Sebastian!!

SEBASTIAN. Cut!

*(Sebastian runs in through the audience again.)*

SEBASTIAN. What do you think you're doing, Brick?

BRICK. What do you mean, what am I doing? I'm doing a scene.

SEBASTIAN. I didn't say 'what are you doing?' I said, 'what are you doing?!'

BRICK. We're speaking English here, aren't we?

SEBASTIAN. Why did you stop?

BRICK. It's in the script. She says her line and that's the end of the scene.

SEBASTIAN. Yeah, but where's my look? My close-up? My pregnant pause?

BRICK. I'm sorry. It didn't call for one in the script.

SEBASTIAN. I see. *(Sighs.)* You're a classically trained actor, aren't you?

BRICK. Yes. I did Chekov off-off-off-off...off... *(Waves indicating 'and so on.')* ...off-Broadway.

SEBASTIAN. Any further off and you'd have been in Jersey. Look, there's a difference between stage acting and soap opera acting. In fact, there's a difference between soap opera acting and any other kind of acting in the world.

BRICK. You lost me.

# ALL MY PASSIONS

BRANDY. *(Snorts.)* And they say I'm dumb!

SEBASTIAN. Try not to prove their point, sweetheart.

*(The comment takes a moment to register on Brandy's face.)*

SEBASTIAN. Okay. Let's pretend we're all actors here.

BRICK. I don't have to pretend. I am an actor.

SEBASTIAN. Great. So we're halfway there. Now ask me a question.

BRICK. What kind of question?

SEBASTIAN. A different one than that. Ask me what I think of Brandy.

BRICK. Okay. What do you think of Brandy?

SEBASTIAN. Hot as a Jalapeño, dumb as a rock. See? That's normal conversation, which is almost like acting, only you don't get paid for it. In normal conversation, someone asks you a question, you answer it. No pause. No hesitation. No meaningful look.

BRANDY. Hey! Did you just insult me?

SEBASTIAN. Sure. But that was twenty seconds ago, and fortunately you were around to hear it.

*(She misses the insult, as he turns back to Brick.)*

SEBASTIAN. Now in soap opera acting, it's not what you say, but how you react. You follow? It's all about 'the look.'

BRICK. The look?

SEBASTIAN. That's right. The look. A worried glance that the camera will zoom in on for a ridiculously long time, just in case anybody in the audience has Brandy's perceptive abilities and misses the fact that we just uttered a significant line. You with me?

BRICK. But isn't that all a bit... cheesy?

SEBASTIAN. No. It's a whole loaf of cheesy. But cheese is what daytime programming is all about.

BRANDY. Hey! Did you insult me again?

SEBASTIAN. When?

BRANDY. About a minute ago?

*(He walks over and kisses her forehead like a little child.)*

SEBASTIAN. Don't ever change, sweetheart. *(To Brick.)* Now ask me the question again, and I'll respond in soap opera acting.

*(Sebastian turns Upstage, his back to Brick and the audience.)*

BRICK. Okay... Hey, Sebastian, what do you think of Brandy here?

*(Sebastian turns slowly and stares with an overly dramatic, soap opera reaction. He holds the pained expression for five full seconds, then slowly raises his hands, palms up and thumbs touching, to indicate a camera frame zooming into his face. Another five seconds, then...)*

SEBASTIAN. And cut! Now that's soap opera acting.

BRANDY. *(Clapping happily.)* Isn't he awesome!

BRICK. But you didn't answer my question?

SEBASTIAN. I will next show. And that scene will start off with you asking the same question again. You see? So whether it's in the script or not, on my soap, whenever a scene ends, it ends with 'the look.' You got that?

BRICK. I think so.

SEBASTIAN. I said...You got that, Brick?!

*(Brick hesitates, then turns dramatically. He does not answer but holds a worried expression for five full seconds. Sebastian uses his fingers to simulate the closeup to Brick's face, then...)*

SEBASTIAN. And CUT! Now you've got it! I'm seeing Daytime Emmy here.

BRICK. *(Pleased.)* I can do this.

SEBASTIAN. If Brandy can, anybody can. *(Running offstage as he says...)* Now, let's pick it up from Brandy's last line!

BRANDY. Okay, Sebastian. I... Hey!

SEBASTIAN. (OFFSTAGE) Yes, I insulted you again, sweetheart. But I still love you.

BRANDY. *(Cheerfully.)* Okay then!

SEBASTIAN. (OFFSTAGE) Let's pick it up pre-orgasm. Brandy's line.

*(The two actors move back to the same position they held at the end of their scene. An intimate embrace, then Brandy pulls away.)*

BRANDY. Wait, Brick. Before we make wild passionate love again... *(Turns her back to him.)* I have something important to tell you.

*(He comes up behind her. Places his hands on her shoulders.)*

BRICK. Something important? That sounds serious.

BRANDY. It is. *(Turning to face him.)* It's... it's about... Dakota's baby!!

*(And this time, Brick gives her a long, exaggerated look of concern. Hold until it is too funny to watch, then...)*

SEBASTIAN. (OFFSTAGE) And CUT! Thanks, Brick. That was perfect. *(Dashes back on stage.)* Actors get out of costume for the group grope scene in Montague's office. And make sure we have enough pancake make-up for Everett's back this time! I don't want to see even one of those um...things again.

*(Sebastian shudders. Brandy and Brick happily cross, Stage Right.)*

BRANDY. So what network is Broadway on?

BRICK. You were cast for your mind, weren't you?

BRANDY. Uh-huh.

*(They exit, just as Newman Forrester leads Hamilton on Stage Left, followed by Melissa, Sebastian, Eric and Wilke, as if they had been watching the previous scene being shot.)*

FORRESTER. So, Mr. Story Editor. What did you think of today's show?

HAMILTON. In a word...reprehensible.

FORRESTER. You wouldn't happen to have a different word on you?

HAMILTON.  I suppose. Cheap. Tawdry. Insulting. Lascivious. Slimy.

MELISSA.  Those were the nicknames of Sebastian's last five wives.

SEBASTIAN.  If you weren't so right, I'd disagree with you.

FORRESTER.  So what's your point, farm boy?

HAMILTON.  We can do better.

FORRESTER.  Do better? Why?

HAMILTON.  Uh...Why?

FORRESTER.  Yes. Why?

HAMILTON.  Because... because we can. Because we can make a show that people want to watch, not ogle over.

*(He looks at the sea of blank faces staring back at him.)*

HAMILTON.  One that brings a smile, not a drool.

*(They're still not getting it.)*

HAMILTON.  Uh... An artistic pleasure, instead of a guilty one.

FORRESTER.  Listen, Mr. High and Mighty, this is what people want. You think PBS scores well with our demographics? Not a chance. Our audience doesn't want its collective mind stimulated. Our audience wants to peer into the sewer. They delight in smarmy.

MELISSA.  Mr. Forrester's right. We have statistics that support that fact.

HAMILTON.  Someone actually gets paid to do statistics for soap opera content? Now there's a meaningful life.

MELISSA.  Sarcasm aside... Our audience is made up primarily of middle to lower middle-class married women. Aged twenty-nine to sixty-four.

WILKE.  They are bored with their lives. Bored with their marriages. Bored with themselves.

SEBASTIAN.  They have obligational sex with their husbands once or twice a month. Yet, they tune in to watch it on TV every day.

WILKE.   We provide them with the excitement they lack in their everyday lives.

MELISSA.   What our viewers really want is to see ridiculously rich and beautiful people be completely and utterly miserable.

FORRESTER.   *All My Passions* represents the sum of their fantasies. An escape from their own lives. You could even say we're providing a public service here.

HAMILTON.   Brandy having sex with half of Seduction City is a public service?

SEBASTIAN.   It was for them.

ERIC.   And it would be for me. Brandy's hot.

*(Brandy runs on-stage, kisses Eric)*

BRANDY.   Thanks, sugar!

*(She dashes back off.)*

FORRESTER.   Besides, it isn't just about sex. She married a whole bunch of 'em.

HAMILTON.   Despite what you may think, I am not completely naive. I understand that people like to escape reality now and then, and fantasy is an easy way to do that. But there are other ways to escape...to uplift...to inspire.

FORRESTER.   I'm not following.

HAMILTON.   I'm simply saying that not all passions are sexual.

MELISSA.   Name one that isn't.

HAMILTON.   Okay...the passion for books.

FORRESTER.   Not a bad idea. Maybe we can have Hustler underwrite an episode if we start flashing their magazine covers.

HAMILTON.   That's not what I meant. I meant the classics. Great thoughts. Reading, you know?

ERIC.   Lust in the library. It could work. We have this horny librarian, who...

HAMILTON.  Excuse me, but what planet are you people orbiting?

FORRESTER.  Planet Nielson. In case you haven't noticed, it's all about ratings. We start having some guy exchanging condoms for classics and the sound of housewives around the country clicking off their televisions would be deafening. Who wants to watch someone reading?

HAMILTON.  There are ways to do it dramatically. You have a couple discussing a book they read. Getting excited about the ideas they've been exposed to.

SEBASTIAN.  Hmmm. He loves her for her mind. That would be different.

FORRESTER.  But who'd believe it?

MELISSA.  You don't think women have minds?!

FORRESTER.  Uh oh. Here we go...

MELISSA.  You don't think it's possible to have a conversation with a woman that doesn't involve sex?

FORRESTER.  I don't think it's possible to have a conversation with Brandy that doesn't involve sex.

MELISSA.  Okay. I'll give you that one.

HAMILTON.  What about food? You can be passionate about cooking. Or music. Or dance.

FORRESTER.  Are you talking stripper chefs? And they call me sleazy.

ERIC.  I could make it work. Fancy restaurant with an 'All-You-Can-Tickle' Buffet. Candles burning. Placemats flying...

MELISSA.  Will someone hose this kid down?

HAMILTON.  If you let me, I can transform this show into something meaningful. Something that matters.

MELISSA.  You can transform the show? Last week, you didn't know a thing about television!

HAMILTON.  But I know about ordinary people, Miss Mulcahey. And I believe your viewers want to be swept off their feet, not swept under the rug. Your audience is not as vapid as you may think.

FORRESTER.  I'll have you know that concept is blasphemy in the television world.

HAMILTON.  Look. I know all the industry attitudes. Write down to your viewers. Assume the average mental age of your audience is twelve years-old.

MELISSA.  Okay, so you know a few buzzwords. We are suitably impressed. But asking us to go out on a limb is just...

HAMILTON.  Just what? Creative? Heaven forbid.

MELISSA.  Being different is different from being right.

HAMILTON.  Of course. No idea can work, unless it's been done before. And once it has been done, it won't work because it's already been done.

SEBASTIAN.  I have that posted in my office.

FORRESTER.  What exactly are you proposing here, farm boy?

HAMILTON.  Shift the focus to love instead of lust. Create a little romance. After all, isn't the anticipation of that first kiss just as exciting as a romp in the sack?

SEBASTIAN.  Only if you're doing it wrong.

HAMILTON.  We've lost the dream. The giggly anticipation. The suggestion of romance. We're in the titillation business now. But it's never enough. That's Newton's First Law of Boredom. The more you show the more you need to show.... What's next? Full copulation on broadcast television?

SEBASTIAN.  Been there. Done that. Won an Emmy.

FORRESTER.  What are you writing, Eric?

ERIC.  Nothing.

FORRESTER.  I saw you scribble something down. What is it?

ERIC.  Nothing, really.

FORRESTER.  Eric?!

ERIC. Well, I was just wondering...does anybody else think 'Copulation' would make a great title for a sexy police series?

*(Forrester bops him on the head.)*

HAMILTON. Listen. I know you gave me this job to shut me up and buy me off. But as I see it, *All My Passions* is a dying show. You've been doing it the same way for so long, even your faithful viewers are starting to desert you.

WILKE. He does have a point there. Our demos show...

FORRESTER. I know damn well what our demographics show!

HAMILTON. You've been inside the fishbowl so long, that you've forgotten there's a whole world with intelligent life outside the glass. Life with a different set of ethics and values.

FORRESTER. So what's the bottom line here?

HAMILTON Give me two weeks.

MELISSA. Two weeks?

HAMILTON. We do it my way for ten episodes. I get control of story line. If it doesn't work after two weeks...if your ratings go down any further, or if there's no change at all...then I'll go home peacefully.

FORRESTER. And drop the boycott?

HAMILTON. Well...

FORRESTER. That's the deal, kid.

HAMILTON. *(Grits his teeth.)* And drop the boycott...

*(Forrester pulls the others into a huddles with the others.)*

FORRESTER. What have we got to lose?

MELISSA. Are you seriously considering turning my show over to a producing virgin?!

SEBASTIAN. Producing virgin? I thought those were extinct out here?

MELISSA. Very funny.

*(As they whisper, Brandy comes up to Hamilton and toys with his tie, making him uncomfortable.)*

BRANDY. I really like what you said about all that, y'know…stuff.

HAMILTON. Um…thank you.

FORRESTER. There's already cancellation talk at the network. Our ratings are down to a two-point-two. This ship is taking on water and I'm ready to try anything.

ERIC. That's it! Why don't we have a character willing to try anything? He's a normal billionaire by day…but at night, he's a polyamorous neo-Nazi pornographer with an armpit fetish…

SEBASTIAN. Fade to black, Eric. Just fade to black..

ERIC. Yes, sir.

*(They break the huddle and turn back to Hamilton. Brandy sees the power shift and starts to flirt more aggressively with Hamilton.)*

FORRESTER. Okay, kid. It's a deal. You got two weeks to breathe life into this corpse of a show. I'm betting you fail, but even if you do, it'll make a great publicity stunt.

HAMILTON. Uh, I appreciate your faith in me.

FORRESTER. No problem. If I can get branded as an innovator, it will help launch my next soap. *All My Perversity*. And Eric, if we get off the ground with that project, I want to talk to you about this polyamorous neo-Nazi billionaire character.

ERIC. Awesome!

*(Forrester, Wilke and Eric exit.)*

BRANDY. This is so exciting, Hamilton!

SEBASTIAN. Come with me, Brandy. This nice boy is not for touching.

BRANDY. *(Cheerfully.)* Okay, Sebastian.

*(Sebastian leads Brandy off. Melissa glares at Hamilton.)*

MELISSA. So, hick boy... you ready to take on the entire studio establishment?

HAMILTON. The question is... is the entire studio establishment ready for me? *(Smiles.)* Listen, Melissa. I know I'm treading on your job a bit, but I really believe we can make this work.

MELISSA. I don't. You can fool Mr. Forrester, but I know what it takes to succeed in this business. And that's a whole boatload of everything you ain't got.

HAMILTON. Maybe. But as Mr. Forrester said, what have we got to lose?

MELISSA. There's always something to lose. That's the first thing you learn in this town.

HAMILTON. Okay. Maybe I do have a lot to learn. I would be happy to listen to whatever advice you're willing to give me. To listen, not necessarily to follow.

MELISSA. Have you always been this pompous?

HAMILTON. I majored in pomposity at Hick High School. Please, Melissa. I would really love to work with you. No animosity. What do you say?

MELISSA. *(Seeing his sincerity.)* Okay...I'll go animosity-free for a day or two. That's all you get.

HAMILTON. That's all I ask... *(Shyly.)* And maybe one more thing.

MELISSA. Why is there always 'one more thing?'

HAMILTON. I was wondering... if you're not um... doing anything right now... Maybe you might think about going to lunch with me?

MELISSA. This is Hollywood, kid. We don't do lunch. We do meetings with food.

HAMILTON. So, uh...is that a yes?

MELISSA. You really are an Opie, aren't you?

HAMILTON. I'm sorry. Could you please hold up a cue card or something? Just so I know when I'm being insulted.

MELISSA. Assume it's continuous.

HAMILTON. *(Turns away.)* Okay. At least I know where I stand... So, back to my initial question... Can an Opie take his cynical, but talented, intelligent and ridiculously attractive producer to a meeting with food?

MELISSA. Are you really for real?

HAMILTON. Help me out here. How is one supposed to answer a question like that?

*(She looks at him like a bug under a microscope, then softens.)*

MELISSA. Okay, hick-boy. I'm willing to see what makes you tick. Lunch is on you, by the way.

*(She exits, Stage Right. Hamilton is left alone on the set.)*

HAMILTON. *(To himself.)* Rampant insanity punctuated by meetings with food... Well, Toto, it looks like we're not in Kansas anymore.

*(Suddenly, an Offstage Voice booms over a loudspeaker.)*

OFFSTAGE VOICE. Toto's out getting his snout lifted and his fur streaked.

*(Hamilton ducks, then looks around in surprise.)*

OFFSTAGE VOICE. Will there be anything else, Mr. Story Editor?

HAMILTON. Uh... no. Thanks... That's fine... Thanks a lot...

*(Deeply embarrassed, Hamilton runs off, Stage Left.)*

OFFSTAGE VOICE. What a loser...

BLACKOUT

## ACT TWO, Scene 1

*AT RISE:  Lights come up on the living room set, where Everett again wears his trademark smoking jacket and toupee. The ice bucket and champagne are again on the piano, signifying that we are entering an Everett/Juanita scene. Everett stares dramatically out the Stage Left window. He does not see JUANITA/WANDA enter from Stage Right, in the same sexy French maid outfit. She is 38, an extremely buxom woman who looks nothing like the first Juanita. The scene looks exactly like the opening scene of the play, only everyone pretends not to notice that a completely different woman is now playing the character of Juanita. Juanita/Wanda pauses, as if surprised to see Everett standing by the window. She hesitates, then says...*

JUANITA/WANDA.  Oh, Mr. Everett. I'm sorry. I...I did not know you were home.

EVERETT.  Actually, Juanita. I was waiting for you.

JUANITA/WANDA.  For me, Mr. Everett?

EVERETT.  Yes, Juanita. Would you like some champagne?

JUANITA/WANDA.  No, Mr. Everett, sir. If Mrs. Everett were to find out...

EVERETT.  You're right. It would not be proper. What was I thinking?

JUANITA/WANDA.  A momentary lapse, sir. A harmless flirtation stopped before it led to... *(Seductively.)* ...unseemly consequences. *(Crosses to him.)* I am so proud of the way you resisted the temptation, sir.

EVERETT.  You are?

JUANITA/WANDA.  Yes, sir. *(Rubs his chest.)* It takes a powerful man to be so strong.

EVERETT.  It does?

JUANITA/WANDA.   A great and powerful man, Mr. Everett. I know now that you have only my best interest… *(Pulls his head to her breast.)* …at heart.

EVERETT.   I…. uh… I… I…

*(Everett stands like a deer in the headlights. His mouth hung open.)*

SEBASTIAN.   *(Entering.)* CUT! What's the matter now, Everett?

EVERETT.   I'm sorry. But shouldn't I be seduced by now? I mean, it is two minutes into the scene and…for some reason…my pants are still on.

SEBASTIAN.   That's right.

EVERETT.   No. I mean, my pants are still on!

*(Sebastian trudges onstage wearily, followed by Eric and his notepad.)*

SEBASTIAN.   And your point is..?

EVERETT.   Don't you get it? My pants are still on!

SEBASTIAN.   I've had that same problem all morning.

*(Everett stomps his foot in frustration, while Juanita/Wanda crosses to the piano and starts guzzling the champagne directly from the bottle.)*

EVERETT.   I am alone in a room with beautiful young Juanita and my pants are still on! Who is possibly going to believe that?

ERIC.   Supposedly, Joe and Mary Trailerpark in Middle America.

EVERETT.   Who?

ERIC.   Ask Hamilton Bennett.

EVERETT.   Hamilton is in charge of my pants?

SEBASTIAN.   In a manner of speaking. *(Sighs heavily.)* Look, Everett. Hamilton convinced Mr. Forrester to take the show in a different direction…

EVERETT.   And that direction involves pants?

ERIC.   You could say that.

EVERETT.  It's my legs, isn't it? I told Cynthia in Make-Up to trim my leg hair.

SEBASTIAN.  Your leg hair is fine, Everett. It's just that we want to let the scene play on.

EVERETT.  Play on?

SEBASTIAN.  Give you time to talk to Juanita here. Get to know her as a person.

EVERETT.  Get to know her as a person?

SEBASTIAN.  That's the idea.

EVERETT.  And why would I do that?

SEBASTIAN.  Why? Because...uh...Because she is your former maid and your future wife. Don't you want to know what she believes? How she feels about things?

EVERETT.  I suppose... How does she feel about leg hair?

JUANITA/WANDA.  *(Raising her champagne glass.)* I'm all for it. Absho-lutely!

*(Wanda hiccups and drinks more. Hamilton enters, Stage Left.)*

HAMILTON.  Can we keep this conversation above the waistband for at least a few minutes?

ERIC.  Speak of the devil. Uh...um, no offense, Mr. Bennett.

HAMILTON.  None taken, Eric. In fact, I'm thinking of having the title 'Prince of Darkness' added to my business cards.

ERIC.  I meant that only in the...uh, 'my-career-laid-to-waste' sense. I'm...um, going to go now.

HAMILTON.  I think that would be wise, Eric.

*(Eric exits, Stage Right. Juanita/Wanda staggers through the door, Upstage Center, still guzzling the champagne bottle.)*

SEBASTIAN.  Let's take five, people!

*(Sebastian exits, Stage Right.)*

EVERETT.  Take five people where?

SEBASTIAN.  (OFFSTAGE) We're on break, Everett! Sheeeesh!

EVERETT.  Oh. Take five..!

HAMILTON.  Which presents me with an opportunity to explain this exciting new spin we have created for your character.

EVERETT.  Does it involve leg hair?

HAMILTON.  You really should consider seeking therapy over that issue.

EVERETT.  Hmmmm.

*(They sit on the loveseat.)*

HAMILTON.  Anyway, about this new spin on Everett Montague. I want you to picture a man...

EVERETT.  Wait! *(Concentrates.)* Okay. Got him.

HAMILTON.  Picture this man as the head of a powerful corporation. Wealthy. Wise. Loved by all.

EVERETT.  Simultaneously?

HAMILTON.  Yes. But not in the physical sense.

EVERETT.  Ahhhh. Interesting...

HAMILTON.  He is loved because of his compassion and understanding for those around him.

EVERETT.  I'm having trouble understanding this 'understanding' thing...

HAMILTON.  He knows what they are feeling. *(Everett is drawing a blank.)* He can sympathize with their needs and fears. *(No reaction.)* He's, uh...read the script synopsis on their motivations.

EVERETT.  Oh, Understanding! Why didn't you say so?

HAMILTON.  People come to him with their problems.

EVERETT.  And he sleeps with them?

HAMILTON.  No. That's the twist. He doesn't sleep with any of them!

EVERETT. I'm suddenly losing the picture of this man...

HAMILTON. Haven't you ever met anyone you looked up to?

EVERETT. There was Ilsa. She was six-foot-five. When I looked up to her, I saw...

HAMILTON. I mean a role model. Someone who had a positive influence on your life? What about your father?

EVERETT. What about him?

HAMILTON. Was he a good man?

EVERETT. My father? Ha! He was a philandering bum who would sleep with anything on two legs. And even that was negotiable.

HAMILTON. Slightly more than I needed to know. But think back, Everett. How did you feel about him?

EVERETT. About my father? How could I feel? I was his seventh child from his sixth wife. I got to see him every other Arbor Day. And then again on Thanksgiving, when he would gather all his ex-wives and mistresses together, along with all his kids, to thank the Lord for his bounty. *(Darkly.)* I wanted to beat him to death with a turkey leg.

HAMILTON. And how many illegitimate children and ex-lovers on *All My Passions* could say the same thing about your character?

EVERETT. Oh, we seldom have turkey here. I prefer ham.

HAMILTON. Why doesn't that surprise me? Okay, Everett. Here's the challenge. I want you to make your character on this show everything your father was not.

EVERETT. Everything my father was not?

HAMILTON. Instead of promiscuous, make him virtuous. Instead of irresponsible, make him strong and dependable. Instead of selfish, make him care about his family.

EVERETT. Everything my father never was.

HAMILTON. And everything your fans can look up to. I believe you can be that kind of man, Everett.

EVERETT.  I can?

HAMILTON.  Do it for your six brothers and sisters.

EVERETT.  Fourteen. I was a middle child.

HAMILTON.  That explains a lot. So what do you say? Is Everett Montague going to be remembered as a man to admire? Or someone who is one day found beaten to death with a turkey leg?

EVERETT.  Ham. I like ham.

HAMILTON.  *(Exasperated.)* Okay. Beaten to death with a ham shank.

*(Everett considers this for a moment, then stands proudly.)*

EVERETT.  I believe I would rather be admired than killed by food!

HAMILTON.  That is the first step on the path of nobility. I'm proud of you, Everett.

EVERETT.  You are?

HAMILTON.  Definitely.

EVERETT.  Do you look up to me?

HAMILTON.  Well, um, I'm starting to.

EVERETT.  I can understand how you would. Excuse me, Hamilton. I think I need to go to my dressing room and be…profound for a while.

*(Everett exits dramatically, Stage Left. He passes Melissa, who enters, Stage Left.)*

MELISSA.  That was nicely done.

HAMILTON.  Excuse me?

MELISSA.  Everett. The way you handled him.

HAMILTON.  I didn't 'handle' him, Miss Mulcahey. I talked to him. There's a difference.

MELISSA.  Not in this town.

HAMILTON. Then maybe letting this town fall into the ocean wouldn't be such a bad idea.

MELISSA. Only if it happens during re-run season.

*(She softens, impressed with his gentleness toward Everett, and the admiring way he continues to look at her.)*

MELISSA. Why are you smiling like that?

HAMILTON. I didn't realize I was. Smiling, I mean. In any particular way, that is... As if I, you know, didn't have a reason to, well, to smile in a certain manner that might be possibly, well, misinterpreted...by you, or anyone else, in fact...*(Giving up.)* I'm sorry. I must have accidentally pressed my idiot button.

MELISSA. Looks like it's jammed.

HAMILTON. You are too kind.

MELISSA. A flaw of mine. So...do all women make you push your idiot button?

HAMILTON. Not all women. Just you...and, well...someone I used to know.

MELISSA. Used to know?

HAMILTON. It was a while ago.

MELISSA. I see.

HAMILTON. You remind me of her in a lot of ways.

MELISSA. She must have been beautiful. Successful. Savagely intelligent.

HAMILTON. She was all of those things...and more.

MELISSA. Why would you be stupid enough to let a woman like that go?

HAMILTON. I couldn't help it. *(Softly.)* She was taken from me.

MELISSA. Someone studlier?

HAMILTON. I'd rather not talk about it, if you don't mind.

MELISSA. Oh, right. A broken heart. How cliché.

*(He smiles softly. She sees the pain in his eyes and chooses not to push it any further.)*

MELISSA. Okay. So why don't you tell me more about yourself, Mr. Hamilton Bennett. I suppose you had the perfect Republican childhood? Nice suburban house. White picket fence. Middle class, college-educated parents. Scruffy dog. Two-point-five children. Barbecues on Saturdays. Church on Sundays. Domestic tranquility ad nauseam.

HAMILTON. Something like that.

MELISSA. I'm not surprised. I knew someone like you had to pop out of a Norman Rockwell painting. It's a lot easier to believe in the good side of life when you grow up in the perfect family.

HAMILTON. Is that what you think? I have standards because my stereotypical sit-com family indoctrinated me with in episode thirty-three?

MELISSA. *(Shrugs.)* Simple philosophies spring from simple upbringings.

HAMILTON. And no one is as simple-minded as a man who believes in integrity.

MELISSA. You said it, I didn't.

*(They stare each other down. After a beat, Hamilton rises.)*

HAMILTON. I guess you got me pegged.

MELISSA. It's a gift. I can spot a happy childhood a mile away. Not all of us were so fortunate, you know.

HAMILTON. I am truly sorry to hear that. You are a woman who deserves happiness.

MELISSA. Thank you. That was extremely close to sincere.

HAMILTON. Closer than you think. But let me give you something else to consider, Miss Cynical Producer…even if the words do come from a 'simple man with a stereotypical childhood.'

MELISSA. And that is?

HAMILTON.  Standing up for what you believe isn't genetic. It's a choice. A choice you make every day.

MELISSA.  Thanks. I'll put that on my screen saver. And maybe I'll look at it every day after you leave us tormented souls and head back to *The Little House On The Prairie.*

*(She regrets the harshness of the barb, after seeing the hurt in his eyes.)*

HAMILTON.  Well, at least it's comforting to know I had some small impact.

MELISSA.  Look, I'm sorry. I didn't mean that to be as cruel as it came out.

HAMILTON.  Oh? And how cruel did you mean it to be, Miss Mulcahey? Now, if you'll excuse me, I think I'll go to my dressing room and be slightly less than profound for a while.

*(Hamilton exits, Stage Right. Melissa starts to go after him, but hesitates, thinks better of it. She turns to see Everett standing beside her.)*

MELISSA.  And what are you looking at?

EVERETT.  I'm sorry, Miss Mulcahey. I was hoping you had a moment.

MELISSA.  I'm extremely busy, Everett.

EVERETT.  Ah.

*(He turns to leave. She sees the disappointment in his face. The second man she has cut down and dismissed in as many minutes.)*

MELISSA.  *(Sighs.)* Maybe I could spare a few minutes, Everett. What is it?

EVERETT.  I was hoping to get your opinion on something.

MELISSA.  My opinion?

EVERETT.  A woman's perspective, if you don't mind.

MELISSA.  Everett Montague, in all the years I've known you, this is the first time I've ever heard you care about what a woman thinks.

EVERETT.  Is that so? That is rather sad, don't you think?

MELISSA. Sad, but typical. You're a man.

EVERETT. I have noticed that about me.

MELISSA. *(Wearily.)* So what do you want my opinion about? Are you unhappy with your wardrobe? You want another Juanita? Wanda is our fourteenth.

EVERETT. Nothing like that. It's just… *(Pauses, looks stunned.)* She is not our original Juanita?

MELISSA. No, Everett. Let's focus on your problem.

EVERETT. Not a problem really. More of a philosophical question.

MELISSA. A philosophical question?

EVERETT. Do women really like to know something about the men they sleep with?

MELISSA. Not really. It complicates things. I prefer not to even know their names. I usually just ask them to take a number.

EVERETT. That would be sarcasm, if I am not mistaken.

MELISSA. Yes, it was. I'm sorry. But why would you even ask me such a question?

EVERETT. Oddly enough, it was something in the script that started me thinking. I suspect it was that Hamilton's influence.

MELISSA. Hamilton? He started you thinking about how to treat a woman?

EVERETT. Not the physical way, of course. I have been in the business long enough for that.

MELISSA. Yes. The first thing they teach you in this industry is how to screw people.

EVERETT. I believe that would be sarcasm again.

MELISSA. You're right. I'm sorry. A leftover defense mechanism from childhood.

*(Everett sits beside her.)*

EVERETT. Mine was delusions of grandeur. Can you imagine?

MELISSA. Not at all. But to answer your question. Yes, some women want to know a man before we open ourselves up. To know him intimately, before we become intimate with him.

EVERETT. And that may take longer than one date?

MELISSA. Can you believe it?

EVERETT. I had no idea...

MELISSA. Everett, haven't you ever wanted to get to know a woman before you married her?

EVERETT. Not really. Although there was this one...but that was many years ago. *(Notices Melissa looking at her watch.)* But I am sure you are far too busy to care about the memories of anyone in your cast.

MELISSA. I'm sure I can spare a few minutes.

EVERETT. You are just being kind.

MELISSA. Spill it, Everett!

EVERETT. As you wish...

*(Everett continues, happily. He is suddenly like a child, remembering his favorite Christmas present.)*

EVERETT. It's funny. I can remember her voice to this day. She had the most amazing vocal tones. Clear, yet velvety. As if she caressed your name with every word she uttered.

MELISSA. What was her name?

EVERETT. Ah. Now you're asking me to really tax my memory. Melanie? Mindy? Monica? No, those were my ex-wives... Melissa? No, that's you.

MELISSA. Thanks for remembering.

EVERETT. ...Eleanor...Eleanor Sweitzman!

MELISSA. And you loved this Eleanor Sweitzman?

EVERETT.   Heavens no. Well, maybe... *(Sadly.)* Perhaps I would have, if I only had a little more time with her.

MELISSA.   What happened, Everett? Did she die?

EVERETT.   She chose a career outside the industry.

MELISSA.   Virtually the same thing.

EVERETT.   It was forty-nine years ago. I was so focused on becoming a star. It was my destiny, and I refused to let anything get in the way.

MELISSA.   And she tried to?

EVERETT.   Not at all. She was my biggest fan. It's just that an actor on the rise must devote himself entirely to his career. Eleanor demanded more of me than I had to give.

MELISSA.   Time?

EVERETT.   Compassion. *(Smiles sadly.)* How strange. I haven't thought of Eleanor Sweitzman in years. Yet, in some ways, she has never left my mind. Don't you find that strange?

MELISSA.   No. I find it very sweet.

EVERETT.   Really? I don't believe I was ever written to be sweet. Sophisticated, sexy, statuesque. But never sweet. How odd.

MELISSA.   Everett, can I ask you something?

EVERETT.   Of course. You are the producer.

MELISSA.   What do you really think of our Mister Bennett?

EVERETT.   I believe he is a character far more complex than he is written to be.

MELISSA.   That's an interesting way to put it.

EVERETT.   And I believe he is quite smitten with you.

MELISSA.   Really?

EVERETT.   Take it from someone who's had seven wives and thousands of affairs. I know a crush when I see one.

MELISSA. You think he likes me?

EVERETT. No. I think he loves you. It was in his eyes the first moment he saw your face. His whole expression lit up with happiness. I almost envied him for it.

MELISSA. You mean, like love at first sight?

EVERETT. More like a flash of recognition. Like he had fallen in love with you once before. Then suddenly, here you were again.

*(Melissa looks off to where Hamilton had exited.)*

EVERETT. It's not like you and I know love, of course. I believe this Hamilton fellow believes in that perverse, old-fashioned, forever-and-a-day brand of love. The kind that drives divorce lawyers crazy.

MELISSA. What do you think I should do?

EVERETT. I believe one should always be courageous enough to embrace the wind whenever it blows new hope in your direction.

MELISSA. Why, Everett Montague! I had no idea you were such a poet.

EVERETT. I'm not. That was dialogue from 1992. Episode nine thousand, four hundred and twelve, if I remember correctly. We had good writers then.

ERIC. (OFFSTAGE) I could have written that!

MELISSA. *(Calling to the wings.)* Shut up, Eric!

ERIC. (OFFSTAGE) Well, I could have...

MELISSA. Look. You know how much this job demands. I don't have time for anyone in my life right now.

EVERETT. Perhaps. But I also believe one should never turn true love into a missed opportunity.

MELISSA. Never turn true love into a missed opportunity. That's lovely. What episode was it from?

EVERETT. None. It was original.

ERIC. (OFFSTAGE) I could have written that, too!

MELISSA & EVERETT. *(Together.)* Shut up, Eric!!

ERIC. (OFFSTAGE) Well, I could have...

EVERETT. Miss Mulcahey, if you don't mind my offering a piece of advice... Eleanor Sweitzman was my missed opportunity. Don't let Hamilton Bennett be yours. Believe me, you don't want to be sitting here fifty years from now wondering what might have been...if only you had gotten your priorities straight.

*(She leans over and kisses him gently on the cheek.)*

MELISSA. Thank you, Everett. It was really good talking to you.

EVERETT. Of course. Shall we sleep together now?

MELISSA. I don't think so.

EVERETT. Ah, well. Old habits are hard to break.

MELISSA. I'm starting to see that.

*(She watches him stroll off, Stage Left. Hamilton enters, Stage Right.)*

HAMILTON. I'm sorry. I didn't know you were still here.

MELISSA. Believe me, if it wasn't for the hundreds of thousands of dollars they pay me, I wouldn't be.

*(He takes it wrong. Assumes she's attacking again. So he nods, then turns to leave.)*

MELISSA. Mr. Bennett!

HAMILTON. Yes, Miss Mulcahey?

MELISSA. I've been thinking about what you said. About standing up for what you believe not being genetic. About it being a personal choice.

HAMILTON. And?

MELISSA. There may be some slight, minuscule bit of truth to that. But what if what you believe is different from what I believe? You want to restrict what's on TV, while I believe in free speech.

HAMILTON. Then stand up for your own beliefs. I would expect nothing less. And hopefully, we can discuss things with an open mind. Maybe even come to some kind of mutual understanding.

MELISSA. The world doesn't operate that way. Especially these days.

HAMILTON. I know. But that doesn't mean it shouldn't. People can disagree about things and still be friends or even coworkers. Or is that too simple a philosophy for you?

MELISSA. *(An apology.)* 'Simple' is such an overused word these days...

HAMILTON. I don't know. I seldom use it. I usually wait to have it applied to me.

MELISSA. Unjustifiably so, I'm sure.

HAMILTON. Do you realize that is the closest you have ever come to offering me a kind word, Miss Mulcahey?

MELISSA. Well, compliments are not on my job description.

HAMILTON. I'm starting to see that.

*(He takes a step towards her. Now it is her turn to be uncomfortable. She is not used to anything other than total control.)*

MELISSA. Anyway, I just wanted you to know that you might not be entirely idiotic.

HAMILTON. That's very generous of you.

*(She hesitates, stares deeply into his eyes. A moment passes between them. A significant one, and they both sense it, before Melissa pulls back, embarrassed.)*

MELISSA. I'm not saying you're right, though...

HAMILTON. I'm starting to see through that.

SEBASTIAN. (OFFSTAGE) Okay, people. Let's get back to business. We've got a soap opera to shoot!

HAMILTON. *(Softly. Lost in her eyes.)* We've got a soap opera to shoot.

MELISSA. *(Softly. Lost in his.)* So I've heard...

*(Sebastian enters, Stage Right, catching their love-struck expressions.)*

MELISSA.  But I better go and do something...um, producerish.

HAMILTON.  I understand.

MELISSA.  Good. *(Turns away.)* Because I have no idea what the hell I'm talking about!

*(She stomps off, Upstage Center, muttering to herself. Hamilton smiles as she leaves.)*

SEBASTIAN.  Am I seeing what I'm seeing?

HAMILTON.  That depends. What are you seeing?

SEBASTIAN.  Is the Hollywood ice princess starting to melt over the Midwest choir boy?

HAMILTON.  Never underestimate the choir boys.

*(He exits happily, Stage Right.)*

SEBASTIAN.  Never underestimate the choir boys... Wasn't that the name of a transvestite musical that opened last year?

*(He follows Hamilton off, Stage Right. After a beat, Hamilton sneaks back onto the empty set through the Upstage Center door. He looks around to see if anyone is watching, then pulls out his iPhone. Dials.)*

HAMILTON.  *(Into phone.)* Pamela? This is Ham... Yeah, it's going great. Better than I could have hoped. I'm on staff now and they've even given me my own apartment. I told you I could pull it off! Hey, you won't believe it, but I actually met someone who looks like she could be Joanna's sister... Yeah, she's really something... Don't worry. You know I never mix business with pleasure... Of course! Really, it would be no problem at all. Come stay with me. There's plenty of room... Great. I'll see you soon... Love you too, Pamela.

*(He exits Upstage Center. After a moment, Eric enters Stage Right.)*

ERIC.  Hmmm... Never underestimate the choir boys.

BLACKOUT

# ACT TWO, Scene 2

*AT RISE: Lights come up on the living room set. The candelabra has replaced the ice bucket and champagne to indicate a Brick & Brandy scene. Brandy enters, Stage Left. Her hair pulled back into a severe bun, and she wears glasses and a conservative business suit. Brick enters, Stage Right. He wears a T-shirt with the slogan, "Save The Sea Horses!"*

BRANDY.  Oh, Brick!

BRICK.  Oh, Brandy!

*(They take a step towards each other but remain a room apart.)*

BRANDY.  Nice shirt.

BRICK.  We all have to do our part. How was your day at the nonprofit center?

*(She pulls out a bobby pin, letting her hair spill freely with a single, seductive shake of her head. She casually tosses her glasses on the loveseat and loosens the top three buttons of her blouse. She is transformed into the sexy Brandy once more.)*

BRANDY.  Exhausting. All those poor homeless people without any homes. But all the time I was ladling out that generic slop to those sweet disgusting bum-types...all I could think about was the taste of your lips.

BRICK.  Oh, Brandy!

*(They rush to each other's arms.)*

BRANDY.  Oh, Brick... A day of charitable giving can be an eternity to people in love.

BRICK.  Sweetheart, when you run your fingernails along my chest, I feel...I feel like I've been... *(Turns to the audience.)*...Touched By An Angel.

BRANDY.  Oh, Brick. Can there truly be a heaven for people like us?

*(They passionately paw at each other. Then start tearing at each other's clothes. Hamilton enters, Stage Left.)*

HAMILTON.   Excuse me... but, what is all this?!

SEBASTIAN.   *(Enters.)*   Cut! What's the problem now, Hamilton?

HAMILTON.   This! They're groping again!

*(Eric and Melissa enter.)*

SEBASTIAN.   You need them to get naked faster?

HAMILTON.   I don't need them to get naked at all!

*(Only on that line do Brick and Brandy stop kissing. They look at the others in confusion.)*

ERIC.   But we changed the script to reflect your family values. Didn't you catch all my references to angels and heaven?

HAMILTON.   Yeah. That was subtle with a capital 'S.'

ERIC.   Thanks! *(To Sebastian)* Told you he'd fall for it.

HAMILTON.   Throwing in a few buzzwords as they jump each other's bones is not exactly what I had in mind.

*(Forrester enters Stage Right.)*

FORRESTER.   What the hell more do you want, Bennett?! You can't completely factor out the horniness quotient. If anything, we are already three affairs and two orgies behind *General Brothel*.

HAMILTON.   There's actually an infidelity equation in daytime television?

FORRESTER.   What can I say? Sex sells.

HAMILTON.   But where does it end? Brick sleeps with Brandy. Everett has an affair with Vera. Brick and Brandy seduce Juanita... There's no bottom too low.

FORRESTER.   Brick and Brandy seduce Juanita... Hmm. That's not bad.

ERIC.   I can write it into the story line in an hour, sir.

HAMILTON. No. I was making a point here. Or trying to anyway.

BRICK. Excuse me... are you done with us?

SEBASTIAN. Yeah. Take five, you guys. *(Sees the exasperation in Hamilton's face.)* Better make it twenty...

BRICK. *(To Brandy.)* Want to rehearse the seduction scene in my dressing room?

BRANDY. *(Cheerfully.)* Okay.

> *(They scamper off happily. Sebastian and Melissa plop down on the loveseat. Forrester sits on the piano bench as Wilke hands him another double espresso.)*

HAMILTON. Look, you all say you do this for the bored housewives of America? Well, I think you're wrong... You do this for yourselves, because you are the ones who are so completely and utterly bored.

FORRESTER. Listen, kid. I'll have you know that boredom is not in my vocabulary.

SEBASTIAN. *(To Melissa.)* Probably because it's a two-syllable word.

HAMILTON. With all due respect, sir. Even the greatest thrill becomes boring when it's always in your face. How many rides on the roller coaster can you take before even that becomes stale?

ERIC. Are you talking about the roller coaster at Disneyworld, or the one at Universal Studios?

HAMILTON. I'm talking about life. The roller coaster is a metaphor.

ERIC. What's a metaphor?

SEBASTIAN. To keep cows in.

FORRESTER. So this is a farming concept?

HAMILTON. It's not a farming concept. It's a wake-up call! *(Earnestly.)* Look at you... You've all done so much yet feel so little. Nothing shocks you anymore. That's why you push the envelope on outrageous behavior. But past a certain point, even the envelope begins to tear.

MELISSA.  I see where you're going with this, Hamilton. But our focus groups tell us...

HAMILTON.  Your focus groups tell you doodly squat!

MELISSA.  Doodly squat?

SEBASTIAN.  A politically correct synonym for excrement.

MELISSA.  Thank you, Mr. Thesaurus.

SEBASTIAN.  No problem.

HAMILTON.  What I'm saying is, I don't think you don't know your audience at all. You only know the empty part of yourselves.

FORRESTER.  Listen, kid. I only let my therapists talk to me like that!

WILKE.  This is getting rather personal. Mr. Forrester doesn't do personal.

HAMILTON.  Think of your viewers...they're the ones who get up in the morning to the same fat slob lying in the bed beside them every day. The same fat slob whose been there for twenty-five years. He's overweight, his breath smells, and he doesn't have half as much hair as he used to. But he's been good to them. He's reliable. He's goes to work even when he's tired. He's understanding even when he's angry. And for the most part, he's faithful even when he's tempted. These women look at their pitifully ordinary husbands and make the hard choice of staying put. They stay together when All *Their* Passions could fit inside a contact lens case with room to spare. It's a choice they make every day. They are the true America. Not its prettiest, or richest, or most fascinating...but its real side. And you aren't doing them any favors by 'focus-grouping' them into something you can manipulate and profit from. You have as much understanding of their hopes and dreams and fears as I have of pederasty!

SEBASTIAN.  *(Dryly.)* Mr. Forrester has a book you can borrow on that subject.

FORRESTER.  Where's all this leading, kid?

HAMILTON. Your beautiful people need to be replaced every few seasons, and somehow...everyone pretends not to notice. My people...the ones who are beautiful on the inside... never get a chance to disappear. *(Choking up.)* Because when they do, others notice. They notice and get hurt. Hurt for life...

FORRESTER. Consequences for negative behavior? That's not bad. Why didn't you think of that, Eric?

ERIC. I did, sir. I had in development, prior to treatment.

HAMILTON. Don't take it to treatment... Take it to heart! *(Desperately.)* *General Brothel. Another Twirl. The Cold and The Pitiful. The Hung and the Breastless. The Guiding Lie...* These are your fantasies, and you sell them to your audiences right alongside ambulance-chasing lawyers and overpriced feminine hygiene products. And believe me, even I recognize the irony of putting those together!

FORRESTER. You sound like you believe this crap.

HAMILTON. If I didn't, I wouldn't be wasting your time.

FORRESTER. Okay, Mister Holier-than-Santa. We'll try it your way. From now on you have full script approval.

ERIC. What?!

FORRESTER. Work with Eric and do whatever you want with characters and plot lines.

ERIC. You can't be serious?!

FORRESTER. What the hell? The network has all but decided to give us the axe anyway.

ERIC. But...but he's not even Writer's Guild!

FORRESTER. Then pay somebody off. And Bennett...

HAMILTON. Yes, Mr. Forrester?

FORRESTER. Try to channel some of that passion you just showed into what's left of my show.

HAMILTON. Yes, sir!

ERIC. But Uncle Newman..?

FORRESTER. I told you, never call me that in public!

*(Forrester stomps off. Eric chasing after him.)*

MELISSA. Congratulations, Hamilton. The speed you keep moving up in this business, someone might think you were sleeping with someone.

HAMILTON. Someone would be wrong.

SEBASTIAN. Well then, someone better get writing, because we're already two hours behind!

HAMILTON. I'm on it.

*(He starts to run off, then turns to face them both.)*

HAMILTON. I have to know... Did any of that register at all?

*(Looking at his face, so eager for approval, even their long-held cynicism begins to wane.)*

MELISSA. More than I wanted it to.

SEBASTIAN. You done good, kid.

HAMILTON. Thanks!

*(Hamilton dashes off, happily. Sebastian turns to Melissa.)*

SEBASTIAN. Am I dreaming, or did Opie just make himself mayor of Mayberry?

MELISSA. He can be pretty convincing all fired up like that.

SEBASTIAN. Easy, Melissa. That little boy's lifestyle is not even in your dictionary.

MELISSA. Maybe it's time I got a new dictionary.

SEBASTIAN. Don't tell me you're really falling for the choir boy?

MELISSA. Me? I don't have time for relationships. And besides, I'd get bored with all that hayseed integrity...in say, forty or fifty years.

SEBASTIAN. I guess even cynics like us can get smitten on occasion.

*(Their eyes meet. There's a lot more to this gesture than he can admit. Years of affection unspoken. He leans in, as if he's about to kiss her. At the last moment, she pulls back.)*

MELISSA. Uh, Sebastian…

SEBASTIAN. *(Catching himself.)* Sorry. Guess I got carried away with that whole 'forever' fantasy he spun. Forgot my place in the post 'MeToo' world. It won't happen again.

*(He starts to exit. Turns to her.)*

SEBASTIAN. I guess some of us are doomed to remain cynics forever.

*(He smiles sadly, then exits, Stage Right. Melissa is left alone, trying to assess this newfound discovery of Sebastian's feelings, just as she finally realized her affections for Hamilton. As she ponders this, a woman in a slinky and expensive dress saunters on from Stage Left. PAMELA is 35, African-American, and extremely attractive and sophisticated.)*

PAMELA. Excuse me.

MELISSA. Can I help you?

PAMELA. I hope so. Can you tell me where I might find Hamilton Bennett? I hear he's the Story Editor around here.

MELISSA. He used to be. Now he's the new Head Writer.

PAMELA. That sounds like my Hamilton. He sure does move fast.

MELISSA. Your Hamilton?

PAMELA. I could tell you stories about that boy that would make your hair turn red. Or whatever color it used to be.

MELISSA. Is that so? *(Melissa extends her hand.)* I'm Melissa Mulcahey. The producer for *All My Passions*.

PAMELA. Pamela Kingsley. Lost visitor.

MELISSA. His office is down the hall on the right. So I take it you know Hamilton well?

PAMELA.   Nobody knows him better. After all, I slept with that boy for years. Let me tell you, that is the only man I know who can snore in three octaves. And don't fall you for that little 'angel on earth' act of his. I could tell you stories... *(Looks at her watch.)* Uh-oh, I've got a meeting downtown in about an hour. So I have just enough time to plant a kiss on Hammy and run.

MELISSA.   Hammy...

PAMELA.   It's been fun chatting with you. Did you say down the hall on the right?

MELISSA.   I'll walk you there. On the way, you can tell me more about our little 'Hammy.'

PAMELA.   No problem. I do so love to get that boy in trouble.

*(Melissa leads Pamela off, Stage Left.)*

BLACKOUT

# ACT THREE, Scene 1

*AT RISE. Lights come up on the living room set, where the ice bucket is again placed on the grand piano. Only this time, it holds a quart of milk in place of the champagne bottle. Everett again wears his trademark smoking jacket and stares dramatically out the Stage Left window. He does not see JUANITA/PAULINA - the latest actress in the role, enter from Stage Right. She looks nothing at all like the two previous Juanitas but wears the same revealing French maid's outfit. Once again, the scene plays out, as if we are not supposed to notice there is an entirely different woman playing the role. Juanita/Paulina pauses, as if surprised to see Everett standing there. She hesitates, then says...*

JUANITA/PAULINA. Oh, Mr. Everett. I am sorry. I did not know you were home.

EVERETT. Actually, Juanita. I was waiting for you.

JUANITA/PAULINA. For me, Mr. Everett?

EVERETT. Yes, Juanita. Would you like a glass of...of low-fat milk? *(He can't believe he's saying this.)* It has great nutritional value, you know.

JUANITA/PAULINA. Oh, Mr. Everett, sir. Even in the midst of your emotional turmoil, you still watch out for my welfare.

EVERETT. We are all our brother's keepers, Juanita.

JUANITA/PAULINA. But I thought the state was your brother's keeper? Ever since he was put in an institution after being driven mad by internet pornography.

EVERETT. Yes. The temptations of demon technology were too much for him. Yet one should not judge lest we be judged.

JUANITA/PAULINA. You still believe that? Even after being nominated for Supreme Court Justice?

EVERETT. I go only to help others. You see, Juanita... I have repented my sinful ways, and now devote my life entirely to serving my fellow man.

JUANITA/PAULINA.  And woman.

EVERETT.  And woman. That is why I have opened the Everett Montague Home For Wayward Girls. *(Grins.)* After all, I helped make so many of them wayward in the first place.

JUANITA/PAULINA.  Oh, Mr. Everett. You are such an inspiration to me. That's why I have come to tell you some important news.

*(DRAMATIC MUSICAL STING.)*

EVERETT.  Important news? Should I be sitting down?

JUANITA/PAULINA.  You are sitting down, Mr. Everett.

EVERETT.  Then I should stand. *(He does so.)* Tell me, Juanita. What is your important news? Are you in some kind of trouble?

JUANITA/PAULINA.  No trouble, Mr. Everett. In fact, I have never been more fulfilled.

EVERETT.  Then what is it, child?

*(He comes up behind her. Places his hands on her shoulders.)*

JUANITA/PAULINA.  This is my news...

*(Paulina takes an old-fashioned nun's cowl out of her bag and pulls it over her head. She turns to face him - a nun from the neck up, though she still wears her sexy French maid's outfit from the neck down.)*

EVERETT.  Good heavens!

JUANITA/PAULINA.  Exactly.

EVERETT.  Juanita, you...you have joined some bizarre, fashion challenged street gang!

JUANITA/PAULINA.  No, Mr. Everett. I have decided to join a convent.

EVERETT.  A nun?

JUANITA/PAULINA.  Yes. I've joined The Little Sisters of Seduction City. I take my Holy Orders next Thursday. Right after Little Muffy has her emergency heart, lung, kidney and spleen transplant.

EVERETT. A nun. I...I don't know what to say...

JUANITA/PAULINA. Just give me your blessing, Mr. Everett. It is because of you that I went and got me to a nunnery. *(She takes his hands as they look into each other's eyes.)* I have seen your spiritual conversion and decided that I, too, needed to repent of my lustful ways.

EVERETT. Ahh. The sin of lust. I remember it well.

JUANITA/PAULINA. So do I.

*(They both look down and share an overly long and wistful SIGH.)*

EVERETT. Yet lust has wreaked havoc on our lives for far too many years. From now on, I seek only love.

JUANITA/PAULINA. And I seek only purity. *(Muttering.)* Should be quite a challenge...

EVERETT. Sister Juanita... *(Touches her cheek.)* I couldn't be any prouder if you were my own sister.

SEBASTIAN. (OFFSTAGE) Grandchild, Everett.

EVERETT. My own daughter...

SEBASTIAN. (OFFSTAGE) Grandchild, Everett!

EVERETT. My own...uh, grandchild.

*(He leans in to kiss her.)*

SEBASTIAN. (OFFSTAGE) On the forehead, Everett.

*(He hesitates, then kisses her forehead. She smiles gratefully. He kisses her forehead again, then again. Then starts to flutter kisses down her neck.)*

SEBASTIAN. (OFFSTAGE) Just the forehead, Everett! Just the forehead!!

*(Everett sighs, gives her one last peck on the forehead.)*

EVERETT. There now. You go off to celebrate your sisterhood and practice a life of celebrity.

JUANITA/PAULINA. You mean celibacy.

EVERETT.  If you must.

JUANITA/PAULINA.  But I feel so awful leaving you alone like this, Mr. Everett. What will you do without me?

EVERETT.  Me? I will to try to patch things up with the seventh Mrs. Montague.

JUANITA/PAULINA.  The seventh Mrs. Montague? Which one was that?

EVERETT.  I'm not sure... Her name was Marla, I believe. *(Counts on his fingers, then nods.)* Yes, Marla... Anyway, there may yet be a flicker of undamaged love which still burns in her desiccated heart. I must make the effort to rekindle the romance. *(Dramatically.)* Or die in the angry ashes of what might have been.

JUANITA/PAULINA.  Poor, Mr. Everett.

*(She moves to console him. He shoves her a bit too hard across the room.)*

EVERETT.  Go now, Sister Juanita. Before temptation leads me to sin against the cloth.

JUANITA/PAULINA.  Yes, sir. And God bless you, Mr. Everett.

*(Though the room separates them, they each slowly raise an arm toward each other with cheesy longing. Hold on their dramatic pose, until...)*

SEBASTIAN.  *(Entering.)* And CUT! Good job, everyone. Take twenty while the crew sets up for the homeless shelter dance number.

*(Sebastian exits, as Hamilton bounces onto the set, happily.)*

HAMILTON.  Wonderful job, Paulina!

*(Once off-camera, Juanita/Paulina's mannerism and voice change to that of a New York street thug.)*

JUANITA/PAULINA.  Yeah, thanks, my ass! I had a good gig goin' here. You show up and...BAM!...I do a sister act and get written out of the whole friggin' show. Thanks for nothin'!

HAMILTON. It's not like that at all, Paulina. We're opening up a whole new story line, where you come to the aid of some troubled inner city kids. Sort of a *Sister Act* meets *Straight Outa Compton*. We can string it out for months.

JUANITA/PAULINA. Yeah? Okay, sweet.

*(She stomps off, Stage Left. Hamilton crosses to shake hands with Everett.)*

HAMILTON. Great job, Everett. That was really quite moving.

EVERETT. Really? It all felt a bit...forced to me. I mean, do people really talk like that? And if so, what keeps them from gagging on their own intestines?

HAMILTON. As I see it, the pendulum on this show has to swing the other way for a while. To make up for the excesses of the last forty-nine seasons.

EVERETT. But Juanita as a nun? Does that mean I won't be able to sleep with her?

HAMILTON. Pretty much.

EVERETT. Damn.

HAMILTON. Look at it this way, Everett. You are becoming a role model for a whole new generation of fans.

EVERETT. A whole new generation? Do you think my fan mail will increase?

HAMILTON. Well, I can't really say...

EVERETT. ...because it has slowed to a trickle over the last few decades. If it wasn't for the Shady View Nursing Home in East Poughkeepsie...

HAMILTON. Trust me. The new Everett Montague will continue to win the hearts of loyal viewers across the country. *(Carefully.)* And in a few episodes, we may even let your hair go natural.

EVERETT. This is my natural hair.

HAMILTON. It's a toupee, Everett.

EVERETT. *(Stunned.)* You knew that?

HAMILTON. Everybody knew that. Sorry, but it's true.

EVERETT. Do you think my viewers knew I wore a toupee?

HAMILTON. Only the ones who watched the show.

EVERETT. So by natural, you mean..?

HAMILTON & EVERETT. *(Together.)* Bald.

EVERETT. I see.

HAMILTON. They will still love you, Everett. If you really care for someone, you learn to overlook their flaws and imperfections.

EVERETT. But my hair...?

HAMILTON. Beauty is only skin deep. And love reaches deeper than any hair follicle.

EVERETT. I sincerely hope you are right, Hamilton. Though I must confess, I am having a little trouble with this integrity thing. It is a lot harder than I had imagined.

HAMILTON. Welcome to the human race, my friend.

EVERETT. *(Confused.)* Wasn't I part of it before?

LIGHTS DIM

*(A SPOTLIGHT picks up a news-desk, Down Right. Dallas Pittsburgh again introduces SOAP OPERA TODAY, with his trademark flawless hair and too-perfect smile. Begin cheesy THEME MUSIC.)*

DALLAS. What the holy hell is up with *All My Passions?* Good evening, America. I'm Dallas Pittsburgh, and that's our cover story on *SOAP OPERA INSIDER*... It has proven to be the biggest shock to daytime television since Donald Trump's on-air proctology exam. *All My Passions*... America's longest running soap opera, has gone from titillation to self-deprivation. Promiscuity to promise keeping...

MORE

DALLAS. (CONTINUED) Even aging Lothario Everett Montague has suddenly realized he's more Grumpy Old Man than wrinkled Romeo. It looks like all of Seduction City has got religion, as *All My Passions* has traded in the bedroom for the Bible... Raunchiness for Romance. In the past week alone, sex-pot Juanita has joined a convent...studly Brick Bannister is poster child for the New Celibacy Movement...and even Vera's Brothel has turned into the Everett Montague Home For Wayward Girls! The result is pure camp, yet strangely refreshing. And sex? Forget it! Characters now talk about love *with their clothes on!* This seemingly suicidal strategy for a struggling soap has transformed it into the hottest property on daytime television. According to the latest ratings, audience members are tuning in with a vengeance. Stay tuned for an interview with Eric Needleworth, the eighteen-year-old writer who single-handled transformed *All My Passions* into the most moral soap on TV. Stay tuned...

> *(MUSIC FADES and SPOTLIGHT DIMS as the news-desk is rolled off, Stage Right. Lights come up on Melissa, who paces furiously, Downstage Left. Sebastian, as always, is trying to calm the situation.)*

MELISSA. That creep! That sleezeball! That liar!

SEBASTIAN. Who are we talking about?

MELISSA. That hypocrite!

SEBASTIAN. Oh. Hamilton.

MELISSA. He comes across all Boy Scout and Snow White, with his innocent charm and candy-coated purity...

SEBASTIAN. Calm down, Melissa.

MELISSA. And all the time, he's shacking up with that rich bitch! And she's older than he is!

SEBASTIAN. Gee, that never happens in Hollywood.

MELISSA. I can't believe I started to... *(Catches herself.)* I can't believe that he suckered the rest of you like he did.

SEBASTIAN. *(Wryly.)* Yeah. Hamilton did a real number on us.

MELISSA. I don't even understand the attraction! I mean, what does he see in that woman?

SEBASTIAN. You want me to start at eye level? Or should I just list her attributes alphabetically?

MELISSA. Okay... so she's gorgeous. And with the jewelry and the way she dresses, it's obvious she's got money and style.

SEBASTIAN. And they have that interracial thing going on, which always plays well in the ratings.

MELISSA. That's all he is, isn't he? Hamilton Bennett is just another real life soap opera. All that talk about 'Middle American values' was just a con job to win himself an instant TV career. How could I have been so blind?!

SEBASTIAN. Don't you think we should hear his side of the story? Before the public execution, I mean?

MELISSA. What for? I have had more than enough guys lie to me. This one just hurts a little more than the others.

SEBASTIAN. I'm sorry, Melissa. I really am.

MELISSA. Don't be. My whole life, you've been the only man who has never lied to me.

SEBASTIAN. *(Softly.)* Thanks for finally noticing.

*(A pause. Hamilton enters from Stage Left. Sees the affection between them.)*

HAMILTON. Hope I'm not interrupting anything?

MELISSA. *(Jumping up.)* What if you were, huh? What if Sebastian and I were about to make wild, passionate love right here on the loveseat?!

HAMILTON. Then I'd suggest we tell the crew to take another five.

SEBASTIAN. Hmmm. Good line.

HAMILTON. Thank you.

SEBASTIAN.  I think this would be a good cue for me to go back to my director's chair and do something...um, directorish.

*(Sebastian escapes, Stage Right. This leaves an uncomfortable moment between Hamilton and Melissa. She crosses to the piano. He pretends to look for dust on the Tiffany lamps.)*

MELISSA.  So... How's Pamela?

HAMILTON.  Terrific. It's funny. She's been all over the world, but this is her first time in Los Angeles.

MELISSA.  She sure has the look of someone who's been around.

HAMILTON.  Excuse me?

MELISSA.  I said, how long is she going to be in town?

HAMILTON.  We're not sure. A week, maybe longer. I've had her move her stuff into my apartment until she decides what she's going to do.

MELISSA.  So you two are living together now?

HAMILTON.  Sure. We usually hook up whenever she's in town.

MELISSA.  You really are scum, aren't you?

*(He is confused by her sudden fury.)*

HAMILTON.  Help me out again. The way I answer that would be...?

MELISSA.  Yes. Definitely. Affirmative to the 'Nth' degree I, Hamilton R. Bennett, am scum! Better than that, I am pond scum! Even better, I, Hamilton R. Bennett, am the scum that forms on the walls of your shower when you don't clean it for a few thousand years!

HAMILTON.  Soap scum?

MELISSA.  Industrial strength soap scum. Mixed with mildew!

HAMILTON.  I'm getting the impression that I've annoyed you in some way. Is it an L.A. custom to tell me what I'm supposed to have done? Or do I have to read about it in the trades?

MELISSA.  Don't get cute with me, hick-boy! I've seen your cute, and I have no intention of falling for it again!

HAMILTON.  Melissa... I hate to see you this upset.

MELISSA.  You ain't seen upset yet, buddy! By the time I reach upset, you best be far away from the blast area!

HAMILTON.  I don't even know what I did wrong?! Look...I care for you. And I don't want you to be...

MELISSA.  Don't lie to me! I'm through letting guys like you lie to me!

HAMILTON.  It's not a lie. I have feelings for you... Strong feelings... And I was hoping...imagining actually...that maybe there could be something between us?

*(Their wildly conflicting emotions, as well as their positioning on stage, subtly suggests they are trapped within their own personal soap opera. In fact, they mirror Brick and Brandy's posturing in this scenes.)*

MELISSA.  The only thing I want between you and me, Mr. Hypocrite R. Bennett, is three bodyguards and half a continent. You got that?!

HAMILTON.  No, I don't 'got that.' I tell you how I feel, and you cut me off at the knees. What is all this?! Huh?!

MELISSA.  What? You say you have feelings for me and expect me to melt or something? No way in hell, hick-boy!

HAMILTON.  You don't believe me?

MELISSA.  Give me one good reason why I should?

HAMILTON.  Because I don't lie. And because...I...I think I might be falling in love with you.

MELISSA.  Yeah. That's original.

HAMILTON.  It is for me. Unlike people in this town, I don't say it that often.

MELISSA.  Not even to the chick who's moving into your apartment?

HAMILTON.  Pamela? What's the girl I'm living with have to do with my feelings for you?

*(A pause as she lets that line sink in.)*

MELISSA. Congratulations. With that line, you're gonna fit in perfectly here in Tinseltown.

HAMILTON. Wait a minute... You think Pamela and I are...?

MELISSA. I don't care to hear about it! In fact, I don't care at all! You are a fictional character! A fabrication!

HAMILTON. Melissa...

MELISSA. You're a phony, Hamilton! A fake! A fraud! A f...

HAMILTON. Run out of 'F' words?

MELISSA. Believe me, I have one more.

HAMILTON. So do I. How about 'foster' child?

MELISSA. What?

HAMILTON. Foster child. My mother was a pregnant teenager. When I was two, she left me in the self-help section of the local library.

MELISSA. *(Shocked.)* She abandoned you?

HAMILTON. It was the kindest thing she could have done for me.

MELISSA. Hamilton, I...

HAMILTON. I know. Nobody feels comfortable hearing about abandoned babies. But it happens. And for some reason...it happened to me.

MELISSA. All that's beside the point...

HAMILTON. Let me finish... I bounced around the foster care system until I was seven. One home after another. Every time I began to feel I belonged, I got yanked out by the courts and thrown someplace else. Finally, this wonderful couple took me into their home. James and Louise Kingsley.

MELISSA. Kingsley?

HAMILTON. James and Louise. Who took a lot of criticism from their black friends for taking in a white orphan. And a lot of abuse from the whites around town for raising a boy outside of their own race.

MELISSA. Let me get this straight... Are you saying you were raised a poor black child?

HAMILTON. When there's love around, you don't notice color. And James and Louise Kingsley had more than enough love to spare.

MELISSA. That would make Pamela your...

HAMILTON. Sister. Foster-sister actually, but they never treated me like anything other than their own child. And I never felt like I was anything but part of their family.

MELISSA. So that's why she said she slept with you?

HAMILTON. Pamela said that? *(Shakes his head.)* That girl does love to get me in trouble. Always did. *(Smiles.)* Yes, we slept together. Same room until I was ten. Different beds, of course. The Kingsleys didn't have a lot of money. That is, until Pamela's first book came out. After that, she bought her parents a mansion.

MELISSA. Her first book? You mean she's *The* Pamela Kingsley? The Prize-winning novelist?!

HAMILTON. I just call her Pamela. When I call her 'The Pamela,' she tends to get uppity.

MELISSA. How stupid do I feel?

HAMILTON. There's no right way for me to answer that, is there?

MELISSA. I thought you two were...

HAMILTON. I guess we do come from completely different worlds, Melissa. If I met some friend of yours, I wouldn't immediately assume you were jumping his bones.

> *(Hamilton realizes how convoluted the situation had become. And how much Melissa must care. They close the space between them. Warmed by his smile, Melissa moves from shock to renewed infatuation.)*

MELISSA. Is Indiana a real place, or is it just a fantasy?

HAMILTON. It's a fantasy. With corn. Lots of corn.

MELISSA. And is everyone there like you?

HAMILTON. Not everyone. Just the phonies, fakes, frauds and f...

MELISSA. Don't say it! I'm sorry I doubted you.

HAMILTON. Don't let it happen again. It might put a crimp in our relationship.

MELISSA. So we have a relationship?

HAMILTON. Maybe...I was hoping...I mean, if you might...

MELISSA. There goes your idiot button again.

HAMILTON. I'm sorry. It's just that when I think of you...or you and me..., if there is maybe a possibility of you and me becoming a...you and me, actually... and I...

*(She leans in and kisses him.)*

SEBASTIAN. (OFFSTAGE) On the forehead, Melissa. Just the forehead.

MELISSA. Shut up, Sebastian.

*(They kiss again.)*

SEBASTIAN. (OFFSTAGE) Now can we please get some work done today?

HAMILTON. I...uh, better get back to writing.

MELISSA. And I'll get back to my...um, producer-thingees.

*(They slowly break apart and exit to opposite sides of the stage. A beat, Eric and Sebastian enter Upstage Center. Eric scribbles furiously.)*

SEBASTIAN. You get all that?

ERIC. Every word.

SEBASTIAN. Well, type it up fast. We've got a show to produce!

ERIC. I'm all over it!

*(They run off, Upstage Center.)*

BLACKOUT

# ACT THREE, Scene 2

*AT RISE. Lights come up on the living room set. The candelabra again replaces the ice bucket on the piano, indicating a Brick and Brandy scene. Brandy enters, Stage Right, dressed like Melissa in the last scene. Brick enters Stage Left, dressed like Hamilton. Brandy turns to him.*

BRANDY.   Oh, Brick! How could you?!

BRICK.   Oh, Brandy! I couldn't. I mean, I didn't! Did I?

   *(They step toward each other.)*

BRICK.   Besides, what does the girl I'm living with have to do with my feelings for you?

BRANDY.   Brick, you are a phony! A fake! A fraud! A f...

BRICK.   Did you run out of 'F' words?

BRANDY.   Believe me, I have one more.

BRICK.   So do I. How about 'foster' child?

BRANDY.   What?

BRICK.   Foster child. My mother was a pregnant teenager. When I was two, she left me in the rubber novelty section of the local adult bookstore.

BRANDY.   She abandoned you?

BRICK.   It was the kindest thing she could have done. I bounced around the foster care system, in one home after another. That led to a life of petty crime, arson and sexual indiscretions.

   *(They play the scene comically similar to Hamilton and Melissa, only with far more cheesiness.)*

BRICK.   I was in the fast lane on the road to ruin, and there was no off-ramp to salvation for me.

BRANDY.   Oh, Brick. I...I never knew!

BRICK. Neither did I. At least until the amnesia wore off. Finally, these wonderful people took me into their home and adopted me. Rufus and Wilhelmina Kingsford.

BRANDY. Rufus and Wilhelmina Kingsford? You mean you were raised a poor black child?

BRICK. When there is love around, you don't notice color. But yeah, I had that cool interracial thing going on.

BRANDY. So that would make your female roommate your...

BRICK. Step-sister.

BRANDY. And that's why you slept with her?

BRICK. It was the Midwest. Things were different back then. *(Comes up behind her, starts to caress her shoulders)* But ever since I started my sex-addiction therapy, I've learned that women are not merely soft, warm, enticing... *(Getting carried away.)* ...luscious, curvaceous...

BRANDY. Uh, Brick...

BRICK. ...nubile...inviting...

BRANDY. Brick!

BRICK. *(Catches himself.)* ...I've come to see that women can be people too. Some with feelings and opinions that could possibly matter.

BRANDY. Oh, Brick. I am so sorry I ever doubted you.

BRICK. Don't let it happen again, Brandy. It might put a kink in our relationship.

*(She moves to kiss him. She starts to rub his chest. Suddenly, Brick pulls back.)*

BRICK. No. We should wait until after the wedding.

BRANDY. Oh, Brick! You really are a new man!

*(She leans her head on his shoulder and he pats her with affection. Hold on this freeze, until Sebastian enters and yells...)*

SEBASTIAN. Cut! That's a wrap! Let's close it up for the weekend, people!

*(Brick and Brandy exit, Stage Right. Sebastian exits, Upstage Center. After a moment, Hamilton and Melissa enter, Stage Left.)*

MELISSA.   Is it me, or did some of that dialogue sound vaguely familiar?

HAMILTON.   All except the 'life of crime' and 'sleeping with my sister' parts.

MELISSA.   Things don't change overnight, Hamilton. Not even for you.

*(They share a smile, which is interrupted when Forrester and his constant appendage, Wilkie, storm on from Stage Right.)*

FORRESTER.   There you are, Bennett! Melissa!

MELISSA.   Mr. Forrester. I thought you were in Washington lobbying for free speech.

FORRESTER.   Free speech, hell. You know how much cash I had to spread around to those politicians?

WILKIE.   Perhaps it would be better if we didn't discuss your Washington contributions so openly, Mr. Forrester.

FORRESTER.   Yeah. You're right, Wilkie. You two forget I said that.

MELISSA.   Said what?

FORRESTER.   You're good, Melissa. That's why I want to keep you on as my producer next season.

HAMILTON.   Next season? I thought the network was going to pull the plug on *All My Passions*?

FORRESTER.   Haven't you seen the latest ratings? We're a hit!

WILKIE.   Ratings are up over three hundred percent! The network changed its mind in the midst of all that free publicity.

FORRESTER.   They even upped our licensing fee! Your romance shenanigans worked! *The Puffington Host* is calling me the pioneer of a new type of soap opera/social comedy hybrid. *Variety* wants to do an entire spread on me. Newman Forrester - TV visionary...or something like that.

HAMILTON.  You must be very proud.

FORRESTER.  Hell, I know you had a little something to do with this, Bennett. That's why I'm making your position permanent.

HAMILTON.  Thanks, but no thanks. This was all very...educational, but I have a real life to get back to.

FORRESTER.  No, you don't. Tell him, Wilkie.

WILKIE.  Mr. Forrester has already arranged to have your studio apartment sub-let.

HAMILTON.  He did, what?!

WILKIE.  He's also contracted with a moving company to have your furniture, tacky as it may be, transported out here.

HAMILTON.  But what about...?

WILKIE.  Oh, yes. We also arranged to have your kitty cat flown out on our corporate jet. Aquinas should be here by six. A limo will meet him at the airport.

FORRESTER.  A limo for your cat. Ha! Only in Hollywood!

HAMILTON.  *(Flustered.)* What gives you people the right to completely disrupt my life like that?!

FORRESTER.  Money, kid. An obscene amount of it. Right, Wilkie.

WILKIE.  Very obscene, Mr. Forrester. Very obscene.

FORRESTER.  And besides... I'm not the only one thinking of disrupting your life. Am I, Melissa?

HAMILTON.  Now listen here, Mr. Forrester...!

FORRESTER.  Call me Newman. But don't call me until the day after tomorrow! I've got places to buy and people to browbeat. You kids play nice now!

*(Forrester and Wilkie disappear offstage before Hamilton can say another word.)*

MELISSA.  I hear they used his personality to design the formula for caffeine.

HAMILTON.  I can't just abandon my life, Melissa!

MELISSA.  You don't have to. Most people out here fly somewhere else for the weekends. The big actors have ranches in Wyoming, penthouses in New York and two hundred year-old estates in Connecticut. I hear we single-handedly keep the airline industry in business.

HAMILTON.  But I don't belong here! I don't fit the lifestyle. I don't drink. I don't smoke. I don't buy bottled air. I don't do plastic surgery as a hobby…

MELISSA.  Then don't. Be yourself. And who knows? You might even end up being a good influence out here.

HAMILTON.  You think so?

MELISSA.  You were on me.

HAMILTON.  Really? *(Overwhelmed by it all.)* So what do you think will happen to them?

MELISSA.  Who?

HAMILTON.  Brick and Brandy. They looked like they were about to start a new phase of their relationship. How do you think it will go?

MELISSA.  Hard to say. At first, Brandy will be a little stubborn. A bit short-tempered. She doesn't handle change very well.

HAMILTON.  I noticed.

MELISSA.  Of course, Brick can be a real pain in the ass too. So arrogant and self-righteous. Especially since he kicked his sex addiction.

HAMILTON.  But Brandy will stick by him, won't she? No matter what?

MELISSA.  Only time will tell.

HAMILTON.  That's not much of a guarantee.

MELISSA. There are no guarantees, Hamilton. A lot depends on how much Brick is willing to open up to her. And how much he's willing to overlook.

HAMILTON. I think Brick is so much in love with Brandy, he's willing to do whatever it takes to make their relationship work.

MELISSA. That's good to hear.

HAMILTON. Of course, there can be no drama without conflict. Happy people make for boring television.

MELISSA. Oh, there'll be drama. You can count on that. But I think Brick and Brandy should be able to weather the storm.

HAMILTON. I hope you're right. Because Brick is expecting a long, long run with this show.

MELISSA. So is Brandy. Maybe for the first time in her life.

HAMILTON. So, um... Just to be clear, we are not really talking about Brick and Brandy, are we?

MELISSA. How can you be so cute and still so clueless?

HAMILTON. It's a talent. Something I have to work at every day.

MELISSA. No doubt. So, hick-boy, what do you say we head out and have a meeting with food?

HAMILTON. Sounds good. I'll have my people call your people.

MELISSA. They're not invited.

*(They cross to the Stage Right door. He holds it open for her.)*

HAMILTON. After you, Miss Mulcahey.

MELISSA. No, after you, Mister Bennett.

HAMILTON. I insist.

MELISSA. Move your ass, Hamilton!

HAMILTON. Yes, ma'am.

*(They exit, Stage Right. Sebastian enters slowly, his eyes lingering where Melissa and Hamilton walked off. He drops on the sofa, dejectedly.)*

PAMELA.  They make a cute couple, don't they?

*(Pamela enters. Sebastian tries to cover his sad expression.)*

SEBASTIAN.  Who?

PAMELA.  What do you mean, who? I thought you were supposed to be the perceptive director. I'm talking about Hamilton and Melissa. They make a real cute couple.

SEBASTIAN.  *(Shrugs.)* If you're into cute.

PAMELA.  And what are you into?

SEBASTIAN.  Emotional self-mutilation, it seems…

PAMELA.  Let me guess… You were the producer-lady's best friend for years, but never told her how you really felt about her. Now it rips you up inside to see that she finally found something real. A chance for love that just might work out in this screwed-up town.

SEBASTIAN.  You know, when most people say 'Let me guess'…they usually follow it with something short and sweet.

PAMELA.  Well, I'm not most people. I'm not short and I'm not sweet. *(Sits beside him.)* And I'm not finished either. So as I see it, you're all torn up, because you don't know whether to be happy for your friend…or mad at yourself for being too scared to let her know you wanted in on the game.

SEBASTIAN.  I'm guessing you have that famous 'author's insight' thing going on.

PAMELA.  No. I have that 'been there - done that, unrequited love' thing going on.

SEBASTIAN.  With Hamilton?

PAMELA.  Are you whacked?! He's my baby brother. And in case you haven't noticed, that boy couldn't be any more white if he came in a milk carton.

SEBASTIAN. So who?

PAMELA. Whom, actually. And I don't make a habit of spilling my love life out to men I just met.

SEBASTIAN. But you have no problem dissecting the crashed and burned love life of strangers.

PAMELA. It's what I do. I thought you might like to talk about it. *(Rises.)* Guess even I can be wrong sometimes…

*(She goes to leave. Sebastian hesitates, then…)*

SEBASTIAN. You weren't…

PAMELA. *(Turning back to him.)* I know. I was just being dramatic.

SEBASTIAN. Uh, I knew that.

*(They share a smile. She sits again.)*

PAMELA. So…Hamilton says you are the one true artist on this show.

SEBASTIAN. Hamilton said that?

PAMELA. He says you've got 'the eye'… Whatever that means.

SEBASTIAN. Well, I call the shots. Try to make caviar out of fish droppings. Sometimes it works, sometimes not.

PAMELA. He also said you might be the perfect person to adapt my latest novel for film.

SEBASTIAN. Your novel?

PAMELA. *Challenge The Wind.* You may have heard of it. Won a Pulitzer Prize a few years back.

SEBASTIAN. *Challenge The Wind?!* I love that book!

PAMELA. I'll send you a signed copy. The studios have been after the film rights for years, but I don't want to sell unless I can find a director who truly understands the characters and the pain they go through.

SEBASTIAN.   I can do pain. I can do lots of pain. I can explain pain. My windows have panes. I even read Thomas Payne. Trust me, pain and me, we go way back…

PAMELA.   I was hoping for a director who could express it a bit more eloquently than that. Anyway, we should talk. Read the book again and maybe we'll toss some ideas around.

SEBASTIAN.   Cool. So, uh, Pamela. How long are you going to be in town?

PAMELA.   I'm not sure. It all depends on what attractive prospects come my way.

SEBASTIAN.   Oh.

*(Long pause. Pamela looks annoyed.)*

PAMELA.   Let me try that again…

*(She turns away, then turns back to him, her voice sultry and dramatic.)*

PAMELA.   I'm not sure… It all depends on what attractive prospects come my way…

*(As she lets the implication dangle, she gives Sebastian 'The Look.' She moves her open hands, thumbs touching, as if they were the camera zooming in for a close up. Sebastian finally 'gets it' and stands.)*

SEBASTIAN.   Miss Kingsley?

PAMELA.   Yes, Mister Evers?

SEBASTIAN.   Could this potential prospect kiss you?

PAMELA.   Let me check my schedule-yes.

*(They share a kiss. Sebastian breaks it off. Looks as if he is judging a fine wine.)*

SEBASTIAN.   Yup. That works.

PAMELA.   Eloquently put. *(Suspiciously.)* This isn't just because you want to direct the film version of my book, is it?

SEBASTIAN. No...but that don't hurt a bit.

PAMELA. Honesty. I like that. You are buying dinner, by the way.

SEBASTIAN. Of course.

> *(They exit together, Stage Right. After a moment, the Upstage Center door creaks open and Everett enters the now empty set. He slowly crosses to a small mirror on the Stage Right wall. He checks again to make sure nobody else is around, drops his coat, then wistfully stares into the mirror. Gradually, as if the act is painful for him, Everett removes his ridiculous toupee.)*

ELEANOR. (OFFSTAGE) It's about time you acted your age, Albert Mooney.

EVERETT. *(Mystified.)* I know that voice...?

> *(ELEANOR enters, Stage Left. She is an elegant, silver-haired woman in her seventies, with a Katherine Hepburn swagger.)*

ELEANOR. I think you look quite distinguished without that lump of roadkill on your head.

EVERETT. Eleanor? Eleanor Sweitzman?

ELEANOR. It's good to see you again, Albert. You are looking well.

EVERETT. Eleanor. It's been...

ELEANOR. Forty-nine years.

EVERETT. I left you on the beach in Santa Monica...

ELEANOR. I remember. I had to hitch a ride home in my swimsuit. I don't believe I ever properly thanked you for that.

EVERETT. *(Amazed.)* Forty-nine years.

ELEANOR. Ever since you first appeared on *All My Passions*.

EVERETT. Eleanor. Eleanor Sweitzman.

ELEANOR. It's Eleanor Abbott now. But thanks for remembering.

EVERETT. *(His face falls.)* You're married?

ELEANOR.   You expected me to waste half-a-century pining over you? I got married two years later to the man who picked me up hitchhiking from the beach. Herman Abbott. We were very happy. But Herman passed away three years ago.

EVERETT.   I am so sorry. *(Brightens.)* Wait. No, I'm not. That means you're single again!

ELEANOR.   So what if I am? Are you planning to dump me on Santa Monica beach again? I'll have you know I'm much too old and wrinkled for a two-piece swimsuit. And my hitchhiking thumb ain't what it used to be.

EVERETT.   No. Never. I'd never leave you on that beach again.

*(He takes her hand and leads her to the love seat.)*

EVERETT.   I have regretted losing you for the past five decades.

ELEANOR.   You didn't lose me, Albert. You made a choice.

EVERETT.   And what has it brought me?

ELEANOR.   Money. Fame. All the women you can diddle.

EVERETT.   Well, there is that.

ELEANOR.   You were born to be a star, Albert Mooney. I always knew that. I just never understood why you believed I would want to hold you back from that.

EVERETT.   I was torn, Eleanor. An actor's life is hard. Unstable. You can be rich one moment and forgotten the next. I felt you deserved better.

ELEANOR.   I wish you had let me make that decision.

EVERETT.   What would you have chosen?

ELEANOR.   I was always your biggest fan, Albert Mooney.

EVERETT.   It's Everett Montague now.

ELEANOR.   Him, I can take or leave.

EVERETT. I simply can't believe I have run into you again, Eleanor. And in my own studio! What are the odds?

ELEANOR. Um...better than you might think. My husband, Herman...God rest his soul...was CEO of your biggest sponsor.

EVERETT. You mean Abbott Laundry Detergent? That Herman Abbott?

ELEANOR. Okay, so I headed up the marketing department and insisted he sponsor your show for the last forty-nine years.

EVERETT. *(Touches her shoulder.)* Did he...did he know about us?

ELEANOR. He knew. He could see it in my face every time you appeared on our TV screen. *(Tenderly.)* But Herman was an understanding man. He was content to have most of my heart.

EVERETT. Most of it?

> *(They stare at each other for a long moment. Decades of separation fade away, and both seem to shed the years with each enhanced heartbeat.)*

EVERETT. I have to ask you another question, Eleanor... Why now? After all this time? Why didn't you...

ELEANOR. Look you up years ago?

EVERETT. Yes. Why did you wait so long?

ELEANOR. Three reasons. The first was that I was married. And unlike you Hollywood people, I took my wedding vows seriously.

EVERETT. I'll have you know I took all my wedding vows seriously.

ELEANOR. All seven of them?

EVERETT. Well, um...

ELEANOR. Which leads us to reason number two... Everett Montague.

EVERETT. Yes?

ELEANOR. No. I mean Everett Montague was the reason. The character you had become. The shallow, sex-obsessed, perpetual adolescent in the flabby, aging body.

EVERETT.  This would be a well-chosen moment to soften that description with a compliment.

ELEANOR.  Yes, it would.

EVERETT.  But you aren't going to, are you?

ELEANOR.  Unlikely. Anyway, as I followed the show all these years, I found it harder and harder to separate the kind, considerate man I knew from the sleazy character he was playing on TV.

EVERETT.  I am an actor. I take on personas. That hardly means...

ELEANOR.  You had your name changed, Albert! Every time you go out, it's always in your Everett Montague wardrobe.

EVERETT.  Well, I...

ELEANOR.  I even heard you had your mansion in Beverly Hills built to resemble this set in every detail!

EVERETT.  *(Defensively.)* Not every detail. The drapes are different. They happen to be a lighter shade of teal!

ELEANOR.  Albert…

EVERETT.  Okay, so they're the same shade of teal! Why are my curtains suddenly an issue?!

ELEANOR.  They're not.

EVERETT.  I walk differently than Everett Montague! Did you know that?! He, I mean me...the character...or me, the actor playing the character. We walk like this...

*(He walks jauntily across the stage.)*

EVERETT.  Now me, me not being the character...we...I mean, me, I walk like this.

*(He walks jauntily back to her.)*

ELEANOR.  Looks the same to me.

EVERETT. You can't be serious! My real life walk has so much more 'intention' to it.

ELEANOR. As I was saying, I kept watching year after year, praying that one day the Albert I knew...the Albert I once looked up to...would somehow reappear. And from what I've seen in the last few episodes, it seems he finally has.

EVERETT. *(Sighs.)* That was mostly Hamilton's doing.

ELEANOR. I know.

EVERETT. You do?

ELEANOR. Your producer called me. She said I should watch the new direction the show was taking.

EVERETT. Melissa called you? How did she...?

ELEANOR. As your leading sponsor, she knew my name. Somehow, she even learned of our history together. I think she was hoping we might still find something in common.

EVERETT. Melissa was plotting with you behind my back?

ELEANOR. Don't be mad at her. It's a producer's job to keep her talent happy. Melissa is very fond of you.

EVERETT. *(Drops to the love seat.)* The world is changing far too quickly, Eleanor...

ELEANOR. No, it's not. You just never noticed it before. *(Sits beside him.)* Time betrays us all, Albert. It's not the Seventies anymore. It's not even the same millennium. I hate to be the one to tell you this, but you are no longer a young star.

EVERETT. Don't you dare tell me I'm old, Eleanor! I can still play a credible romantic lead!

ELEANOR. Only to me, Albert. Only to me. And I'm just an old widow with only a scrapbook of faded memories to keep me warm at night.

*(She lowers her head, wonders if she made a mistake coming here, admitting so much. Tears grace her cheeks. Everett wipes away the tears and raises her chin with a gentle hand.)*

EVERETT. You are not old.

ELEANOR. And you are obviously not seeing very clearly.

EVERETT. Perhaps. Or perhaps I am seeing more clearly than I have in a very long time. *(Takes her hand, gently.)* Eleanor. I mean, Mrs. Abbott...

ELEANOR. Yes, Mr. Mooney?

EVERETT. Would you do me the honor of having dinner with me tonight?

ELEANOR. I'd love to, Albert. *(Sternly.)* Provided you don't think I'm one of these dime store chippies who put out on the first date.

EVERETT. There is more to love than lust, Eleanor. If you watch the show in the coming weeks, you just might realize that.

ELEANOR. Get your coat, Everett Montague.

*(He smiles, grabs his coat, then reaches for his toupee.)*

ELEANOR. That, you can leave.

*(Everett hesitates, then slowly drops the toupee on the loveseat. He takes her arm.)*

EVERETT. Your wish is my command, dear lady.

ELEANOR. Well, it's about damn time.

*(They walk off, arm in arm, through the Upstage Center door.)*

LIGHTS DIM

OFFSTAGE VOICE. You have been watching *All My Passions*, starring Everett Montague as Everett Montague. Join us tomorrow for another episode of America's longest running soap opera, brought to you by Abbott Laundry Detergent. Proud sponsor of *All My Passions* for nearly half a century...

# The End

# All My Passions
## ORIGINAL CAST

| | |
|---|---|
| **Everett Montague** | Charlie Hunter |
| **Melissa Mulcahey** | 34, the show's hard-hitting producer |
| **Sebastian Evers** | 48, the show's frustrated director |
| **Hamilton R. Bennett** | Jim Parker |
| **Eric Needleworth** | 18, the show's latest head writer |
| **Newman Forrester** | James Wolford Hardin |
| **Wilkie** | 48, Mr. Forrester's assistant |
| **Brandy** | Jamie Bratcher |
| **Brick** | 29, The handsome stud |
| **Juanita** | 26, Everett's maid & love interest |
| **Juanita/Wanda** | Patty Owens |
| **Juanita/Paulina** | 19, Juanita's next replacement |
| **Dallas Pittsburgh** | 40, A tabloid TV Host |
| **Pamela Kingsley** | Pattie Golden Crawford |
| **Eleanor Sweitzman** | 67, An old acquaintance |

| | |
|---|---|
| Director | Vin Morreale, Jr. |
| Stage Manager | Erika Wardlow |
| Lighting Designer | Charles Wade |
| Set Design | Bill Baker |

## About The Playwright

Vin Morreale, Jr. is an internationally produced playwright, published author and award-winning screenwriter.

Vin was a founding member of the San Francisco Playwrights Center and the Senseless Bickering Comedy Theatre. He has directed hundreds of works for stage, screen and radio across the country. He was awarded the prestigious *Al Smith Writing Fellowship*, and his scripts, stage plays, documentaries, museum exhibits and radio comedy have received hundreds of productions around the world, as well as being translated into Chinese, Italian, Russian and Spanish.

Vin has sold material to network and cable television networks, had screenplays optioned and produced, and his work has been seen in more than 15 countries. He was named a top screenwriter by both The International Screenwriters Association and TheBlacklist.org.

As president of *Vin Morreale Casting,* along with his nationally known *Burning Up The Stage* acting workshops, he has helped nearly 30,000 actors find work in movies, TV, stage and video.

You can find more of his books and plays at *academyartspress.com.*

## *Also by Vin Morreale, Jr.*

### ACADEMY ARTS PRESS
http://academyartspress.com/shop-for-books

The KISS ME Curse
The Carrie Variations
Forsaken
Captive Christmas
300 Monologues
Two Character Chaos
150 Acting Scenes
Chicken Fat For The Damaged Psyche
Knowing When To Leave
Dark Wilderness & Other Stories
Mabel The Maple
Too Many Rules

### DRAMATIC PUBLISHING
dramaticpublishing.com/authors/profile/view/url/vin-morreale-jr

Burning Up The Stage – *Monologues & Audition Scenes for Actors from 6 to 70*
Breaking & Entering
House of The Seven Gables
Uncool
Nicky's Secret
Southern Discomfort
The Happy Holidays Collection

### ELDRIDGE PUBLISHING
histage.com/search?q=Morreale

The Fairyland Detective Agency
Sonoma White & The Seven Dolts
Fairies, Fantasies & Just Plain Fun

### OFF THE WALL PUBLISHING
offthewallplays.com

Exquisite Anxieties – Seven Slivers Of Suspense
Temp Work
Empathy – A Celebration Of Women's Voices
Ladies Guild Pre-Christmas Planning Session

www.ingramcontent.com/pod-product-compliance
Lightning Source LLC
Chambersburg PA
CBHW071024080526
44587CB00015B/2484